STR
SERVICE,
& SMILES

STRUGGLES, SERVICE, & SMILES

The Autobiography of a Depression Era Kid

God Bless Tony

Bob Wiley

Robert B. Wiley, Lt. Col.,USAF, Ret.

Outskirts Press, Inc.
Denver, Colorado

Outskirts Press, Inc.
http://www.outskirtspress.com

ISBN: 978-1-4327-7433-2

Library of Congress Control Number: 2011929565

Outskirts Press and the "OP" logo are trademarks belonging to Outskirts Press, Inc.

PRINTED IN THE UNITED STATES OF AMERICA

Table of Contents

Foreword

As my four children became adults I realized they knew little about me before they were born. Using a cassette recorder I recounted my early life. I filled both sides of six cassettes.

The next Christmas I sent each child a copy. After my oldest daughter listened to the recordings she called and said, "Dad, you had a crappy childhood." (Her opinion was the original title of this book).

I disagreed and told her that with a few exceptions, all my friends were in the same boat. As Depression era children we lived by "use it up, wear it out, make it do or do without."

In spite of my daughter's perception of my youth I believe in Robert Louis Stevenson's verse, "The world is so full of such wonderful things, I think we should all be happy as kings." I know I always have been, in spite of some childhood trials.

May this book evoke fond memories in my contemporaries.

My Gene Pool

I realized that I knew little about my family before I was born. When I contacted a genealogist I was shocked at the cost. A three hundred buck deposit to start! That was too steep for my billfold so I bought a software program and started on my own. When I got into it became clear that $300 may have been reasonable. This was hard!

I got birth and death certificates. I searched census records at the Denver Federal Center. This led to some frustration when the census taker did things like entering a name "Elmer E." rather than "Elmore." I contacted family members that I found were doing the same thing. I was able to locate my great-grandfather Wiley and learn that my great-great Grandfather on the Dayton side was an immigrant from Germany who lived in New Jersey. I was also able to conclude that most of the Wiley's were farmers with an occasional brick layer. The Dayton's tended to be businessmen, even in an agrarian society.

Age made my eyes start to fail so I stopped the written

research and started to rely on stories I heard from family members. So this is my ancestral tree.

Omer Earnest Wiley was born September 28, 1895, in Somerset, Pulaski County, Kentucky. He was the youngest of three brothers, sons of farmer Elmore Wiley and Dora Lee "of the Virginia Lees." I later found that "Lee" in Virginia is like "Smith" or "Jones" in other parts of the country. Omer was raised by a black "Mammy" who was considered a part of the family, an accepted custom of the time. This relationship may have influenced one of Omer's actions later in his life.

Bertha Iona Dayton was born December 19, 1898, in Brooklyn, Poweshiek County, Iowa. She was the oldest and only daughter, of Perry Adelbert. Dayton was the son of a Civil War pensioner. He would later start the first Buick automobile agency in Grinnell, Iowa. His wife, Edna M. Kensinger, was the third oldest of eleven children of a farm family. It is interesting to note that her mother, after eleven children, divorced her father but that he showed up on a later census as "a hired hand." Edna was an extremely religious person who would sometimes alienate others with her forceful demands that they follow her lead.

Bertha was a bright child and started keeping books for a local grain elevator when she was fourteen. Although she was only five foot five she played on her high school's girls basketball team. She wished to attend normal school because she wanted to become a teacher. Her skills as a speaker put her on the debate team and won her awards in elocution.

Bertha's skills were not limited to academics and athletics. She also played the piano and was mechanically inclined. Her auto dealer father parked a car behind their home when the dealership mechanics were unable to make it run. "Bert" as she preferred to be called and her brother, Harvey, six years her junior; tinkered and tested until they were able to drive the car around the block. Unfortunately, someone reported them to their father who returned the vehicle to the dealership lot. Harvey later became an executive at GM Delco although he had been expelled and never graduated from Grinnell High School. Shortly before the ceremony, he and his friends outfitted the school's statue of "The Discus Thrower" with an athletic supporter.

When Sergeant O.E. Wiley was discharged following World War I, he did not return to Kentucky. He joined his buddy, Howard Dayton, in the home of Howard's father, Harry, in Northern Iowa. Harry, and his brother Perry, were close and their families spent considerable time together. Howard's army friend, Omer, was treated as part of the family and it was only a matter of time until Miss Bertha caught his eye.

After courting for some time Omer became serious, but Bertha was having none of that. She was finishing normal school and nothing would keep her from becoming a teacher. When he became more persistent, she accepted a teaching position in a rural multi-grade one room school near Wray, Colorado. Some of the taller sixth grade country boys towered over her five-foot- five frame but in no time they realized who was boss. In the summer time she was a telephone operator for Mountain Bell.

Not to be deterred, young Omer followed his heart and moved to Colorado to continue his courting.

Finally, love won out and the young couple planned in a romantic moment to be married on Valentine's Day. Young passions burned hot and they decided not to wait. They were married February <u>13</u>, 1920, in Greeley, Colorado.

The newlyweds moved to a farm outside Wiggins, Colorado, a town of about 250 people located approximately sixty miles northeast of Denver.

Although she was a city girl, Bert was not unfamiliar with farming. She had spent many summers on the farms of her several uncles and her Grandma Kensinger.

Because of limited equipment, Omer had to borrow a pitchfork from a neighbor. Unfortunately, he broke it and went to town for a brand new same model replacement. When he returned it to the lender, he was asked what had happened. When Omer replied, the neighbor insisted that if the tool broke that easily, he wanted a better brand. When Omer disagreed, the neighbor responded with, "Wiley, get down off that wagon. I'm going to take the price of a new pitchfork out of your hide!" With the nickname of "Irish," the challenge could not go unanswered.

Following the "discussion" the young bridegroom returned home bloody and bleeding. While she was cleaning him up, the young bride noticed that an ear lobe was missing. She asked, "Where is it? We will take it to the doctor and have it reattached."

His answer was blunt. "I made the son-of-a-bitch swallow it."

Some time later Swift and Company offered Omer the job of managing the cream station in Wiggins. It was the place that all the farmers brought their raw milk. The milk was measured for butterfat content and the producer was issued a check. The milk and cream were separated, placed in five or ten gallon cans and placed on the daily train to Denver.

In the 1920's the Ku Klux Klan was very strong in Colorado. There were a number of black farmers in the area and they, too, brought their raw milk to the cream station. The Klan demanded that the young manager cease serving them. Wiley replied, "Their skin may be a different color, but their milk is as white as yours." A cross was burned behind the station but there was no violence and business continued as usual.

"Hi World, I'm Bobby"

There is at least one doctor who said I shouldn't even be here. Shortly after my parents were married they were warned that because of my mother's physical build, child-bearing could be life threatening.

Because of Omer's burning desire to have a son, they decided to take the risk and I was born as Robert Bernard Wiley on September 4, 1924, in the back of the cream station. After determining that the new mother was oaky, my Dad wrapped me in a blanket and took me across the street to the pool hall to show off his new son to his buddies. My middle name, Bernard, was in memory of my Dad's younger brother who had died as a child.

As I recalled my childhood, I came to a conclusion. In some instances you recall the entire incident. Other times the recall is a specific part of a larger situation. There are times I have no recall whatsoever and rely only what I have been told. I choose to start with one of the latter.

When she wasn't helping in the cream station, my

mother had to maintain the household. Keeping an eye on an active toddler was a challenge. Radio was in its infancy and powerful Denver station KOA only broadcast at night. Other hours there was only static. When I became restless, my mother would turn on the battery operated radio, sit me on the floor and place a headset on my little noggin. I would sit quietly, listening to the noise. Do you suppose that affected my gray matter?

My earliest recollection is of coyotes howling. That can be very frightening for a little boy. Times were hard and the state of Colorado paid a bounty for an animal's two ears and a tail. One resident took advantage of this deal and raised coyotes. Every time a train went through town, the animals in all the pens howled at the same time.

In a small town, everyone knew everyone else and their family. One day when I was about three, I was missing! The search was on. Men stopped work. Women left their kitchens. Everyone looked everywhere. They knew that Bobby and his dog, Ike, were inseparable. If they could spot Ike, Bobby would be somewhere near. Finally, my dad found Ike at the local grain elevator, sitting at the bottom of the ladder leading up to the top of the structure. He just sat there and looked up the ladder. My dad climbed up and found me at the top calmly admiring the view. The only thing I remember about the entire incident was seeing a tractor, way in the distance, throwing up a cloud of dust.

Who could forget the day that he became "King of the Hill?" In addition to managing the cream station, my Dad had a rural mail route. Sometimes I would ride along. I remember seeing the antelope herds scatter as we drove by in the noisy old Model T. On this particular day, the mail had just been placed in the box on the side of the road when a little girl ran down from the house to get it. Suddenly my Dad yelled at her to stop! He had spotted, or heard, a rattle snake at the base of the mail box post. He took the car jack, threw it, and cut off the snake's head. Then came the best part! He took his knife, cut off the snack's rattle and gave it to me! With my very own reptile rattle I became the envy of every kid in town.

My father was an avid hunter and fisherman. Much of our meat was due to his prowess. I remember biting into pieces of buckshot in rabbits, pheasants and ducks, and being warned about the bones in fish that he brought home. Of course, I was much too young to accompany him. Except on one occasion.

My folks and I joined another family on a weekend trip to Loveland, Colorado, which lay at the foot of the Rockies and at the mouth of the Big Thompson River. The group set up camp on the banks of the river, somewhat up the canyon. While the women were laying out the picnic spread, the men started to catch the meal. My Dad handed me a pole, threw a baited hook on the line, and placed me on my tummy at the river bank. Glory of glories, I caught a fingerling. Nothing could convince me that it should be returned to the river. I spent the afternoon admiring my catch in a bucket of river water. The turning point came when I was told that if I kept it until it grew big, we would have to eat it! I couldn't have that, so I reluctantly returned my prize to the River. That was my total fishing experience until some thirty years later.

I was assigned to ferry some senior officers of the Air Defense Command on an inspection trip of bases on the West Coast. One of these stops was Hamilton Air Force Base in Marin County, California, on the north coast of San Francisco Bay. After we landed, a Lieutenant Colonel approached me and my co-pilot and said, "We have made arrangements to do some ocean fishing tomorrow morning and would like to have you join us. Think it over and we will see you at dinner."

I had no interest whatsoever, but my co-pilot pleaded with me, "Please, Wiley, I'd love to go but I can't go with that bunch of wheels by myself." I grudgingly agreed.

The next morning we started out. The boat trip past Alcatraz and the Golden Gate Bridge was great and the Pacific was beautiful. When we were a mile or so off shore, the crew stopped the boat, gave us each a fishing rig. There was the pole, the hook and line, and a heavy metal ball. The ball was to drag the line low in the water and was attached with a device that, when a fish struck, it would release and drop to the ocean floor. Hooks were baited, the lines thrown in the water and we began to troll. I thought it was rather boring, but I did catch one fish. Buddy George got "skunked."

At the end of the day as we approached the home dock,

the lieutenant colonel approached me with a list. He said, "Okay Wiley, we have figured it out. The boat and crew were so much, the guide was so much, the rig rental was so much, the bait was so much, the lost balls were so much, and the cleaning and ice packing will be so much. Here is the total and your share is $55!!"

That amount may not have been much to a lieutenant colonel, but to a young captain with a family it was a blow. That fish (I don't even know what kind it was) was about 16 or 18 inches long and I don't know how much it weighed, but I'd bet it set a world record for price-per-pound!

I met my future at the age of three and a half. An airplane! After the war, some of the men who had flown in World War I decided to continue a life in the air. Some of the lucky ones were hired to fly the mail. Others became what came to be known as "barnstormers." They would fly to a small town, land in an open field and take some of the more adventurous citizens aloft for a fee. My dad was so excited that he could not wait.

And nothing would do except to take his little boy along. What a thrill! I loved the idea of sitting on Daddy's lap and going for a ride. Until the engine started! The roar was bone chilling. My mother rescued me, crying and screaming and took me away from that frightening monster!

The barnstormer visit was out of the ordinary. But there were some regular special events. One was the "turkey shoot." No turkeys were shot, but they were given as prizes to the winners of the trap shooting contests where clay pigeons were the target. The annual event was sponsored by the American Legion and was held on Decoration Day, forerunner of Memorial Day. The same day, the legion auxiliary conducted "Poppy Day." Small paper poppies were sold to raise funds and to honor the dead of World War I. My mother taught me the words of the poem that starts, "In Flanders Field the poppies grow, between the crosses, row on row." My dad was the legion post commander. Years later I mounted his legion post commander medal with his World War I Victory Medal. When I mounted my own wings, drank insignia and medals, I gave them both to my eldest grandson who had served five years in the Marine Corps.

I do not remember my mother "teaching" me anything. They did not call it "home schooling." I know she read to me a lot, mostly poetry. Longfellow works like *The Village Smithy*, *The Song of Hiawatha*, *The Children's Hour*; and one that starts, "This is the forest primeval, the murmuring pines and the hemlocks." There were a lot of works, poems and books by Robert Louis Stephenson. I recollect nothing of numbers, alphabet or spelling. She must have implanted knowledge of these because when I finally did enter school I skipped kindergarten and first grade.

While I watched a Colorado Rockies game on television, I thought back to the Sunday afternoon baseball games in Wiggins. There was a backstop, but no seats. You sat on the ground or you relaxed in one of the Model T Fords that surrounded the field. The crowd noise could be heard in town, but it was nothing compared to the simultaneous honking of those cars with every good play or home run. Sometimes after the game the teams and the towns' people would cool off on a hot afternoon by going out to Jackson Reservoir. I could not swim, but I remember wading and squishing my toes in the mud along the shore.

When I got big enough my first job was in the cream station. The separator was hand operated. It had a huge, heavy flywheel. It made the handle so hard to turn that I could actually hang on it with my full weight and it would hardly move. But after my folks got it started the inertia was enough that I could keep it going with lots of effort.

Swift and Company transferred my father to Denver and we settled in a home at 3836 Wyandotte. About the only thing I remember about that house is that it had a heat register in the hall between the bedrooms. After the coal furnace in the basement was fired up, I could stand on that grate and be warm and toasty on the coldest winter day.

I started school in the second grade at Columbian located at 39th and Federal, close enough that I could walk. School was no big deal, but city life was. Horse drawn wagons delivered bread, dairy products, vegetables and ice. Those horses were so smart that they would stop at the right houses while their drivers walked along the sidewalk! The ice truck was the greatest. Every family had an ice box. They had a square card with a number on each side: 10, 25, 50, 100. On the day the ice man came, they would place the card in a front window with the number on top showing the desired pounds of ice. The ice man chipped off the requested amount from a large block in his wagon, hoisted it up on a leather-covered shoulder and took it in the house. But here is the best part. When he chipped off the block in the wagon, hunks would fall on the street! Fair game for kids! Nothing was better on a hot summer day than a chunk of ice to suck on.

I was growing up. Grown ups drink coffee. Why not me? I began to tease for coffee. I was so persistent for so long that my mother finally consented. But she didn't tell me that she had filled the sugar bowl with salt! That was it. I was off coffee until about thirty years later.

My wife of Swedish descent was a great coffee drinker. A hot pot was nearly always on the stove. I was leaving for a year tour in Iceland when she asked, "Honey, while you are up there, why don't you learn to drink coffee? If you do, I will make your breakfast every morning as long as we are married." That sounded like a good deal so though I hated it, I learned to tolerate black coffee. When I returned home, Mickey kept up her end of the bargain -- for maybe three weeks. But since she was happy that was what mattered. I still drink black coffee but I am not devastated if I don't have a cup in the morning.

Ever since I was little I suffered with a double hernia. When it hurt, I learned to lie on my back and with my small fingers I learned to push my intestines back up into place. After the family moved to Denver, my folks bought me a truss. It was uncomfortable but it held things in place. I learned to avoid activities that caused discomfort.

My folks saved enough money to send me to St. Anthony Hospital to have the condition permanently corrected. The anesthesiologist was one smart lady. She said, "Bobby, this mask is going to smell awful. What you should do is take a big breath and blow the smell away." She was right. It did smell bad. I took a big, big, breath -- and wasn't awake to blow it out.

The procedure was successful, but the recovery was a problem. Why? Because my parents decided that since I was not circumcised in the back of the cream station, it should be done then. Big mistake. I strongly suggest, no urge that parents of a male child have this snipping done as soon as possible after birth. Recovery at age seven was not pleasant.

Recently Congress passed a massive health care bill. The primary provision of this bill, as I understand it, is to require every citizen to have health insurance. Several states are challenging the law on constitutional grounds but I think it is wrong as a matter of principal. The federal government should protect the people, but not from themselves. Some may prefer to just pay for medical care themselves. Others may elect to take the risk. Yes, some may choose to have the insurance. But it is their choice, not that of some bunch of politicians. And another provision of the law, touted as great, is that children stay on their parent's health care policy until the child is twenty-six years of age! Are we going to raise a generation of leeches? These "kids" have been legal adults for eight years, for heaven's sake.

Health care insurance may have been around when I was growing up, but I do not recall any mention of it. Our parents took care of us as best they could or we coped. We endured all the childhood diseases like measles and chicken pox. Most of us escaped polio and scarlet fever. I never had the mumps. Treatment of the common cold was pretty much universal. Mom rubbed my chest with Vicks Vaporub or put on a mustard plaster. For the head cold, a dollop of Vicks was placed on a saucer and it was floated on a pan of boiling water. I put my face over the pan, a towel was hung over my head and the pan, and I breathed the vapors. I was put to bed with lots of covers. The thing that I feared most was to have a severe sore throat. In that case Mother would wrap the end of a pencil with a rag soaked with iodine. She would then swab my tonsils. When I gagged I could taste the iodine. It was awful. In our neighborhood, chicken soup was not included in my treatment.

With the exception of the St. Anthony incident, I do not remember ever seeing a doctor. I never saw a dentist with one exception. I once chipped a tooth while boxing. When I received my draft notice, I spent some of my college money to have the tooth repaired because I was afraid the Army would not accept me.

I feel that health-wise I was pretty lucky as a kid. I never had a broken bone and I never had a cut that required stitches. There were just two problems that persisted. The first was hay fever. Every ragweed season my eyes would ooze matter at night and each morning I would have to take a washcloth and unglue my lashes so I could open my eyes. The sneezing was an annoyance, but nothing more. The other problem was with ingrown toe nails. They were so severe that bloody socks were quite common. An Army doctor used thin pliers and in about two minutes they were out. I am sure that if the pain had become unbearable, my mother would have found a way to pay some doctor to do the same thing.

Dad was laid off by Swift and Company and the family moved to Colorado Springs. I have two fond memories following the move. The first was when I got a red scooter. I was so proud when I learned to coast and balance with both feet on the board. The second was seeing my first sound movie. It was at the beautiful Ute Theater and was a cowboy movie called *Robbers' Roost*. What a thrill!

We lived in a nice brick home on the east side of town. My folks started a business called Pikes Peak Advertising. Neither had any experience in this field and I remember them studying books and pamphlets from ICS, The International Correspondence School. After a time, the business failed and we moved to a frame house on West Pikes Peak. It was located at the foot of the Garden of the Gods and my friends and I had fun playing among the beautiful red rock formations. It was there I got my first pet since my dog Ike, a little horned toad that I never did name.

My father got a job at a gas station. Then a gas pump was a metal structure about five feet tall with a glass cylinder on top that held five gallons of gas. The cylinder had etched marks at the gallon and half gallon levels to measure the amount of gas dispensed. After the sale was made, the cylinder was refilled by operating a pump that pulled gas from an underground storage tank. On occasion, it was my job to operate this pump as my dad checked the oil and tires and washed the windshield for the customer. It was at this station that I began my relationship with tobacco.

I am not proud of it, but one day I snitched a sack of Bull Durham "fixing's" tobacco and a package of cigarette papers. My friend Bobby and I rolled our own and smoked that entire sack in our cardboard clubhouse. Believe it or not, neither of us suffered any ill effects. Maybe if we had, the future might have been different.

I smoked at every opportunity. Butts. Some roll your own. Later when I sold papers on the street, I'd get a pack of "tailor mades." Not the good brands like Camels, Lucky Strike and Chesterfield; but Wings or Victory. I had no trouble buying them "for my father" because what clerk believed that a ten-year-old was buying them for himself?

When things were tough I would smoke coffee. Coffee? Yes, it was a poor substitute, but it was something. How? For a penny you could buy a "Guess What." Inside a paper roll was a piece of candy and a small toy. One toy was a small pipe for blowing bubbles. I put the coffee in the bowl and lit up. No good. When I puffed, the coffee came up the stem. No problem. I just put a piece of cloth over the stem, pushed it into the bowl and puffed away. It worked fine until the burning coffee burned through my cloth. Drawing burning coffee grounds into your mouth is an experience to be avoided.

My adventure continued until I was about ten. One day coming home from school I met a nosy neighbor lady while I was having a smoke break. That night my mother told me that she had talked to the woman and did I have anything to tell her. I admitted my actions, what else could I do?

Mother said, "Honey, I understand. Your daddy smoked and you thought it was all right. But it is not for little boys. Please promise me that you will not smoke until you are out of high school." I made and kept that promise. It was years later that my association with tobacco was renewed.

When my dad lost his job at the filling station, we moved to a property on Wheeler Street near the Golden Cycle Mill. The house in the front was abandoned and had been vandalized. The barn, where we kept a cow and the outhouse were in fairly good condition. Later the location of the outhouse would cause a minor tragedy. We lived in a concrete block building which may have formerly been used as a tool shed or a milk storage facility. We did have running water.

My parents both worked, trying to make ends meet. I was left alone most of the time. I have always had a good appetite and one day that box of All Bran looked very inviting. I stopped eating when I had consumed about half the box. In the middle of the next night, the laxative properties of the bran became apparent. I headed for the outhouse but it was located about twice as far as I had hoped. My pajamas were badly soiled and a little brown trail started about half way to my destination.

About this time I learned a valuable lesson in obeying

my parents. My dad had a set of golf clubs and I asked if I could play with one. Permission was granted but with one proviso; I could use the club only with my rubber ball. Since I was home alone, I thought no one would know if I used a real golf ball. My friend and I went out in the road, made a little dirt tee, placed the ball and I took a mighty swing. I was so proud when the ball took off but, it developed a hook which incidentally stayed with me the rest of my life. That ball sailed across the road and through the window of "that crazy old man."

When my parents got home he came over ranting and raving. He was assured that his window would be replaced. My family was in no position to come up with any cash so they arranged for me to establish a route for the sale of Zano Products. Zano specialized in the sale of coffee, tea, spices and personal care items like soap, tooth paste and an occasional lipstick. Times were hard and selling was difficult. Probably most of my sales were because folks felt sorry for the young salesman, but I got the funds to replace the window.

One day my mother packed our clothes and said we were going to take a trip. A lady showed up and we were off on what I thought was to be a great adventure. Little did I know that I would never again see my dad. I did not even get a chance to say good bye.

It was, indeed, an adventure. There was, evidently, not room for me in the car and I lay in front, wedged between the hood and the fender. What a thrill! The wind blew in my face and hair. I thought I was flying. When we arrived in Sioux City, Iowa, we moved into an apartment with a friend of the driver. It was on Court Street, not too far from Irving grade school and close to the Mary Elizabeth Day Nursery. I was enrolled in both and my mother went to work picking chickens in one of the local packing houses.

Not too long later, we received word that my father died. My Grandpa Dayton picked us up and we returned to Colorado Springs for the funeral. He was buried in the American Legion portion of The Evergreen Cemetery. Many years later when I was stationed in Colorado Springs, I went to the archives of *The Gazette Telegraph* and found the article on my dad's death. He had taken his own life and left a note saying he was disconsolate because his wife had left him and had taken his son with her.

He died on February 13, 1934, my parent's fourteenth wedding anniversary.

Life without a Dad

My nine-year- old mind did not fully comprehend the loss. I had not lived with my dad recently so there was no real shock. On the way back from the funeral, my thoughts were of returning to school and my friends.Life in Sioux City was different.

Of all the kids that I played with, the only one that I remember is Virgil. He was different. Virg had a hunch back and one leg was shorter than the other. I was told that he suffered from "rickets" due to malnutrition. He played hard and even though he could not run as fast as the rest of us, he always tried and kept smiling. I had a great admiration for Virgil and he was a good friend.

In our apartment house the bathroom was at the end of hall. It had the lavatory, a commode and a bath tub. One day

I forgot to lock the door when I took my bath. In walked a strange woman! I was naked! Of course I was in the tub. She couldn't see anything. She just smiled, said "Excuse me," and walked out. But I thought I had been traumatized for life. It was the first time I was completely embarrassed.

For breakfast the normal meal at the Mary Elizabeth Day Nursery was mush. It came in different flavors, but it was mush nonetheless. For lunch we had fried mush, left over from breakfast. That was plenty of incentive to go to work hawking the *Sioux City Journal* down on Fourth Street.

The Journal was on the west end of Fourth. I picked up a bundle of papers and sold them for three cents each. I had to pay the paper two cents each and kept the penny. The bigger, older boys had corners staked out and had semi-regular customers in cars or on foot.

I worked the length of the street from the Milwaukee Grill to Mook's Café. The grill served only hamburgers, hot dogs, chili and pie. Hamburgers were a nickel and my ambition was to save a dollar, plop it down on the counter and say, "Keep bringing me hamburgers until the dollar is used up." Of course, by the time I had a dollar all at once, the price had gone up substantially. Mook's was at the other end of the street. Here I could get a bowl of braised beef and a stack of bread about four inches high for fifteen cents. Fourth Street had stores and a bunch of beer joints. Some of the patrons were sometimes high and would pay a nickel, or even a dime, to the "paper kid" for the three cent paper. On a good night, I could sometimes eat at both ends of the street.

Really, the Mary Elizabeth was not so bad. When we got there after school, we were treated to a slice of bread with some sort of spread. The bread was good, but the method of serving was great. At the time, loaves of bread came wrapped in wax paper. That wrapping was cut into four inch squares to use as serving plates for our slice. After eating, we would take our "plates" out and wax the slide. In our little minds the wax application made a great deal of difference in our rate of descent.

For the first time in my life, my mother told me she was disappointed in me. I had gone to the library and brought home the book about the little engine that could. "I think I can. I think I can." Then, when he reached the top of the hill, "I thought I could. I thought I could."

I thought it was a great story. But my mother said, "Dear, I'm sorry you picked out a book meant for younger children. You can do much better than that." This became my introduction to *Tom Sawyer*, *Huckleberry Finn* and *Boy Scouts of the Air in the Northern Wilds*.

I was in my last year at Irving Grade School. With $600 that she had scrimped and saved, my mother bought the property at 1601 Carlin. The improvements included a house, a hen house, rabbit hutches and an outhouse. The area was known as Kelly Park after the five or seven acre city park about half a block away. The park was all grass except for a backstop and a softball diamond. And SOFTball was an apt description. At times the ball we used was just a sock stuffed with rags. We felt lucky if we found a discarded ball that we could wrap with black tape to hold it together. There were few home runs.

In the winter time, the city would re-grade and flood the diamond to make a skating rink. They also installed a warming house with a pot belly stove. The railroad was not far and we would go down to the tracks and pick up pieces of coal that had fallen from the steam engines. After we got the fire started, it could burn unattended while we, as we got older, skated with an arm around a girl or played a rough game called "Piss Pot."

In "Pot" the ice was divided in two. At each end of the ice was a three foot circle called the pot. Each team's players patrolled within three feet of the center line, moving constantly. Players were supposed to break over the center line and try to reach the "enemy's" pot without being touched. "Touched" may not be descriptive enough. I tried not to be touched, pushed, tackled, tripped or body checked. An NHL skater would have admired some of the hits. If I reached the pot, my team scored a point. If I encountered an opposing player, I was put in the pot and my team could not score until a teammate was able to rescue me by running the blockade. Prisoners could be traded and the game continued until the teams got tired or someone had to go home and do chores.

To say that my athletic skills were "average" may border on exaggeration. But I always played hard and played to win. Wow!

I did win an eight inch basketball trophy. It reads "Wing Headquarters Squadron, McChord AFB Champions, 1950-51, R. Wiley." By the time the trophies were awarded, I had been transferred and a good team mate, Bob Pienowski, forwarded mine.

We had some really good players on that team. One had played college ball at the University of Kentucky. The team needed a guard. I could not shoot worth a hoot but, like I said, I played hard and played to win. I would fight for the rebound or the loose ball in the opponent's end of the court. Today, I would be known as a point guard. I would bring the ball up the court, find the open shooter and pass him the ball. As the game progressed, it became apparent that I was not going to shoot. The opponents dropped off me and double teamed our best players. Toward the end of the game the score was close and neither team was able to put the ball in the hoop. As I brought the ball up, my teammates started to chant, "Shoot, Wiley, shoot."

I hesitated. "Shoot, Wiley, shoot." Finally, I launched one and glory of glories, it went in. I was in shock. The next time down the floor, it was "Shoot, Wiley, shoot." Okay I did. Same result. What a thrill!! By the time the other team reacted to this new "threat," I had picked up a foul and had scored nine whole points! We won the championship and my sole athletic achievement is a fond memory for an old man.

The buildings on Carlin Street were built on a plateau dug out about half way up a fairly steep hill. I don't remember counting them, but there were about a hundred steps leading from the dirt street to a small front yard. The three room frame house was about ten feet wide. The front room was some eight feet deep, the kitchen and eating area six feet, and the bedroom ten feet. The back yard, dominated by the chicken pen, ended at a six foot high dirt wall about twenty feet from the house and the hill continued up from there. The house was heated by an oil stove in the front room. Fuel came from a distillate store in a fifty-five gallon drum. The fuel was siphoned by sucking on a hose until the fluid flowed into a can to be taken in the house. Only practice helped you avoid washing your mouth out with the foul tasting stuff, an act to be studiously avoided.

I really liked living in that home. When I was little I could cuddle with my mother in the freezing back bedroom on a winter night. Later, I slept on a couch in the front room where I could listen to my favorite radio programs. At first I listened to *Let's Pretend* a show where fairy tales were acted out. Then I liked *Jack Armstrong, the All American Boy*, *The Green Hornet*, *The Shadow* and *Inner Sanctum*. But the best of all was one whose name I can't remember. It featured Jack, Doc and Reggie in "Another Carlton E. Morse Adventure thriller." As I grew more, I enjoyed more adult fare with *Lux Radio Theater* and *Grand Central Station* introduced by "Crossroads of a Million private lives." And I still remember Bob Hope, Jack Benny, Fred Allen, and Fibber Magee and Molly. Life was good.

It may seem insignificant to others, but one of the great things in this home was taking a bath! Saturday night, Mother would turn on the oven in the kitchen, bring out the wash tub and partially fill it with hot water and give me my bath. When it was over, she would wrap me in a Turkish towel and scrub me all over until I turned pink. Those rub-downs were a great end to the week.

The door in that kitchen instilled in me a habit that lasts to this day. The outhouse was about twenty feet from the door. During a freezing Iowa winter that was a marathon distance. When nature called with a major item of bodily waste, I would stand at the door and wait. And wait. And wait. When waiting was no longer an option, I would dash madly, finish my business with the softest pages of the Sears catalogue and dash back into the house. I understand that some men take reading material with them into the bath-room. Not I. The kitchen door habit remains. Go, do, done!!

The first Christmas on Carlin Street I got a bike! I am sure that Mother could not afford it and she paid a dollar a week for who knows how many weeks. She did not want the hassle of me changing schools for half a year and I could pedal back to Irving. That bike was my life and part of my livelihood until I graduated from high school when I sold it to buy my class ring.

It was not possible for me to sell daily papers on Fourth Street after we moved from downtown so I sold magazines. *Liberty, Colliers, Saturday Evening Post*, and *Ladies Home Journal*, among others. I had been in offices in the city and almost every one had magazines. What a market! I found out very quickly that most of them had subscriptions. Poof! No market. Then I sold seeds during planting season. Somehow,

I always seemed to have a few cents in my pocket for the essentials like Saturday morning movies at the "Hip."

Sioux City had several movie theaters. They ranged in price from top to bottom as the Orpheus, The Princess, the Rialto, the Circle and the "Hip." I was told that was short for Hippodrome, whatever that was. At the cheapest movie house a dime on Saturday morning would buy a bag of popcorn, a cartoon, a newsreel, a feature (sometimes two) and a serial.

The serial was a short action or western film. At the climax, when the hero or heroine was in dire circumstances the movie would end. To see the rescue I had to come next week. Easier said than done.

In one episode, Dick Tracy was chasing the bad guy over the water. Tracy had the larger and faster boat and was gaining. The culprit darted between the dock and an ocean liner. Tracy followed, but his boat got wedged in the small space. Then the liner started drifting toward the dock. Dick used everything at hand to stop the closing but everything he used was getting crushed. End of serial. Much to my dismay, the next week I was broke and never did know how the rescue came about. I didn't worry about Tracy too much; I still had cowboys Tom Mix and his horse Tony and Ken Maynard with Tarzan. And there were Buck Jones, Johnny Mack Brown and Tom Tyler.

As much as I liked our new home, the house had a major problem. It had no foundation. It had been built on some clay tiles, many of which were cracked or broken. Mother had a friend who was a house mover and he came over and braced and raised the house and we began to excavate the basement. We started with the perimeter for the foundation walls. We dug out an incline and one of us would fill my wagon with dirt and the other pull it up with a rope and dump the dirt on the vacant lot next door.

We worked at this evenings and weekends even though my poor mother was working full time picking chickens in the packing house and came home with bleeding and blistered hands. When space for the basement walls was dug out, I mixed and we poured the footers. When they had cured, Mother started laying up the cinder block walls. It was up to me to bring the cinder blocks, two at a time, either up the steps from the street in front, or down from the hill in back. She would tell me how many blocks I should have ready when she got home from work. When she got home, I would mix the mortar and she would lay up the wall. She left an opening in the wall for a door. I dug out room for steps down from ground level and she installed a stair wall and stairs.

When the foundation wall was finished, the movers removed the support timbers and we were able to complete the excavation. I don't remember how the basement floor was poured since I had nothing to do with it. All I knew was that I now had my very own room. Talk about living high!

The basement was a one time deal, but the garden was an annual event. Each spring Mother would have a friend with a team of horses plow up the lot next door. It was then up to me to rake, level, plant, maintain and harvest. We had all the vegetables that we liked and we could can. Tomatoes, beans, peas, corn and beets. Then, of course, was fresh produce like leaf and head lettuce, cabbage, radishes, potatoes and onions. We also grew a couple of perennials, asparagus and rhubarb.

I liked creamed new potatoes and peas, but most of the other things I could bypass. There were two exceptions. I liked to roll leaf lettuce with sugar and, actually, nothing could compare to sitting in the garden with a salt shaker and eating fresh tomatoes off the vine.

In season, Mother would come home after working all day and she would can until one or two o'clock in the morning. I had no right to complain, but I hated it and swore when I grew up I would never, ever, have a garden.

So much for a vow. Years later, when we had our first home, my wife asked me to put in a garden. There was a nice twelve foot by twenty foot spot next to the house, but I refused.

"Honey, if you will just dig it up, I will do all the rest." How could I refuse? I loved her. So I spaded it up and handed her the rake. She had never had that tool in her hand and it drove me crazy seeing her leave lumps on an uneven garden bed. So I raked. I strung a line between two pegs and handed her the hoe. She was worse with the hoe than with the rake. I tried to teach her to take little strokes and make shallow seed beds. I finished the hoeing. I had to teach her not to drop a pinch of seeds but to plant one seed at a time and cover them lightly. Finally, everything was planted. Then, she announced that she was pregnant with our second child and she would be unable to tend the garden! We did have a good harvest.

My life as a kid was not all work. Far from it. In addition to the park, we had open fields just a few blocks away. It was a great place to pack a potato in mud and bake it in the coals of a forbidden fire.

At Halloween there was no such thing as "trick-or-treat," but we had fun. Some of the older boys knocked over some outhouses. I bet they never had to straighten one up afterward. We had a party at the church and bobbed for apples and played games. We did have fun with one antic. Grant School on 18th stood higher than the street. Opposite the school was another ridge, with the road a valley in between. We would anchor a string on one bank and run it across the road. Then in the middle we would tie a white rag on the string and cover it with dirt. As a car got near, we would pull on the string and the white "ghost" would leap up to windshield height. The frightened driver would slam on the brakes, screech to a halt and we would take off.

Kids today may have their Wii's, but they probably never heard of our "magic box." It was called an orange crate. The box consisted of a frame of two-by-twos with the sides and bottom covered with sheets of wood about one eighth of an inch thick. I could put the crate in my wagon and increase its carrying capacity by three. Or I separated the wheels on a discarded pair of roller skates and mounted them on the bottom of a two-by-four. I turned it over and fastened the crate to the front. I had a vehicle that could challenge a modern day skate board. In winter I could break it apart and use it for kindling in the ice pond warming house.

Have you ever played in a sewer? The main street in our neighborhood had a series of four foot storm sewers. What an adventure to crawl in so far that it got dark and dream of being captured by pirates and placed in a dungeon. How were we going to escape? These were the summer use of the sewers. The real practical use came in the freezing winter when we stayed in the warmth of our underground playground as we waited for the school bus to take us to Woodrow Wilson Junior High School.

It was about this time that I had to do the most difficult, if not the hardest, task ever. I had to dig a new pit for our outhouse. When we dug out the basement, all I had to do was put a shovel full of dirt into a wagon. This job was different. It was not hard when I started because the hole was only about eighteen inches wide and three feet long. By the time the hole was up to my hips, throwing the dirt up became a problem. There wasn't much room to stand and my elbows hit top of the sides. When I was chest deep, it was almost impossible to throw out a shovel full of dirt without dropping half of it back into the hole. Fortunately by the time I was down where my shoulders were at ground level, I was allowed to stop digging since the depth would suffice for as long as we lived there.

Beginning to Grow Up

I really liked the junior high. Elementary school was one classroom and recess. At Woodrow Wilson Junior High we changed rooms and had assemblies. The best part was shop. There were six semesters from the seventh through the ninth grade. The first semester we took woodworking, then electrical, metal working, printing, then mechanical drawing. In the sixth semester we chose our favorite for some more advanced work.

We were required to take general science, algebra and plane geometry. I did okay in those classes but English, History and Geography were more interesting to me.

We also had speaking contests and I remember that Stanley Baron trounced me in the extemporaneous division. I also had a part in the class play and it is like yesterday in my mind that both my friend Frank and I forgot our lines. Believe it or not, we ad-libbed until we got back on script and the audience never knew. The teacher was a nervous wreck.

Life at home was also interesting. We raised chickens and rabbits for both food and sale. We had one big buck and three, sometimes four, does. When each doe delivered, we would sell the females in the litter to hospitals for pregnancy tests and raise the little bucks until they were old enough to butcher. The pelts were turned with the skin side out and stretched over a frame made from a coat hanger. When they were dried, they were sold to the I. Chesen and Sons junk yard for a dime a piece.

Mother bought mixed breed baby chicks because they were less expensive. The producer did not have to separate them. We had some Bared Rocks, Rhode Island Reds, Leghorns and others. The first two breeds were primarily for eating and the Leghorns were the egg producers. I learned to estimate egg production by placing three fingers over the hen's bottom where the ends of the back bones and breast bone were located. If that "delivery point" was relatively small, she became food.

Until the chicks were ready for market they had to be fed. If some of an earlier batch had been sold, there was money to buy food. Until then, it was up to me. We lived fairly close to the railroad tracks where the grain elevators were located. A grain car had two walls. The inner wall had a small opening at the top and bottom to allow air circulation. When grain was blown into the car, occasionally some product would become lodged between the walls. Employees swept out the cars, but did not mess with the grain between the walls. I would take a stick and fish out that grain through the slot in the bottom of the wall. I could pretty quickly retrieve a half a gunny sack full!

After Mother had killed and dressed the chicken or rabbit, she prepared it for sale. The rabbit was just wrapped in wax and brown paper. It was marketed to individual households or a butcher shop.

The chickens were a different matter. If it was a roasting chicken it was cleaned out and wrapped as were the rabbits. The fryers took more work. Mother would cut them in pieces; a breast, two thighs, two drumsticks and two wings with the tips removed. The pieces were placed on wax paper in a paper tray. Then I would ride my bike to the fancy part of town where people paid a premium for fresh eggs and wanted to be pampered with ready to fry meats. The receipts went a long way toward augmenting the meager paychecks. All the entrails and wing tips were fed to the chickens. I think organic farmers would have been proud of me since all of the droppings from the hen house and rabbit hutches were used to fertilize the garden.

About this time, I had a little private business deal of my own. Keeping milk fresh without an ice box was a problem. I had managed to save a little money and I was able to buy a bred nanny goat for five dollars. She dropped two little billy goats, but one was born dead. The survivor was the cutest little brown and white guy that I ever saw. I kept nanny tethered on the hill behind the house, but Billy ran loose since he would not stray far from his mom. I didn't like the taste of goat milk by itself. But it was used in all the cooking. The goat had to be milked every day and what we did not use we fed to the chickens and rabbits.

Not too long after Billy was weaned, a man who wanted to build a goat cart for his little girl saw him. Impressed with his markings, he asked if he was for sale. Maybe. "Would you take four dollars for him?"

I said, "How about five?" We made a deal. I thought that was pretty neat. I had my five bucks back and I still had Nanny. Oddly enough, I can't remember when I got rid of her.

As I thought about the old neighborhood, I remembered our street car. Since we lived past the end of the line and there was no turntable, we had a reversible street car. The conductor would take his controls and change the box to the back of the car which became the front. The backs of the seats were flipped over so they were facing the direction from which the car had come. But most important, the pole that reached up to the overhead wire had to be reversed.

If I was going downtown and was lucky enough to be at the stop when the car arrived, the conductor would allow me to unfasten the anchor device, take it to the other end of the car and reattach it. For this "service" I was allowed to ride free. The conductor was especially grateful in the winter time since he did not have to leave the car.

Unfortunately some of the older ruffians came close to spoiling the whole deal for the rest of us. Sometimes, when the street car was en route, especially if there were girls aboard, they would pull the rope attached to the power pole.

Everything would go dark, the car would stop. When the pole was released it would hit the overhead wire and sparks would shower down. Conductors did not like that.

The little Glendale Baptist Church, the only house of worship in the neighborhood, was the center of the social life we had. It was a small frame building, but it had a steeple with a bell that we boys rang with vigor every Sunday morning. We had no minister, but we had Sunday school every Sunday morning. Sometimes in the evening the Reverend Silas Delmar Huff, minister of the First Baptist Church in Sioux City, would come and preach. On occasion, we would have communion. Even as a sub-teen I wondered why we were served bread and grape juice instead of wine. Jesus even turned water into wine. As an adult I learned that the Pope does not recognize the Archbishop of Canterbury, The Archbishop does not recognize the head of the Eastern Orthodox Church and Baptists do not recognize each other in a liquor store. My mother never attended the evening church service, but she did come to play the piano and lead the Sunday school choir. We had parties, pageants and programs at Easter and Christmas.

It was in the depths of the Depression and there were tough times for everyone. In spite of it all, I continued to have blessings. I always had a warm place to sleep. I always was furnished with serviceable clean clothes. But best of all, I always had plenty to eat. Besides the garden and the meat we raised ourselves every once in a while we could get a one pound can of shredded beef at the welfare office. Sometimes when hamburger was on sale for a nickel a pound we got some. And there was Mr. Gould. He had a corner grocery store just down the hill from our house. Sometimes I would ask him if I could have a piece of liver "for my cat." Of course we never had a cat, but when Mother breaded and fried it with some onions, it made my tummy "purr."

And we were not without desserts. On occasion, if she was not too tired, Mother would bake a pie or cake. I even tried my hand. I once baked a beautiful looking peach pie which had a crust that you could not cut with a knife. We ate the delicious filling. I can tell you from experience that if you fail to put baking powder in your chocolate cake mix, the cake will come out of the oven looking like a brownie. Cookies were no problem. Johnson Biscuit Company had a deal where you could buy a full cookie box for a dollar. The box was about an eighteen inch cube. It was filled with culls, overruns and broken pieces. "Broken" as when the chocolate coating on the marshmallow-topped cookie was slightly cracked. My bike and I made numerous trips down to Johnson's.

I am convinced, beyond all doubt, that my character as a man had its foundation in the time when I was twelve to fourteen-years-old. One summer at vacation bible school, my memory lesson was "First Thessalonians 5:22 tells you exactly what to do." That chapter and verse, in the King James Version, reads "Abstain from all appearance of evil."

In my twelve-year-old mind, that meant you had to be so good that folks would never see you do something that even looked wrong. Then I learned "Good, better, best. Never let it rest. Until your good is better, and your better best."

At church we had to learn the books of the Bible and the Ten Commandments. I thought God had set the bar pretty high when he gave those tablets to Moses, but I would give it my best shot. At fourteen, as was the Baptist custom, I was baptized by Reverend Huff at the First Baptist Church. Scripture says "He who believes and is baptized will be saved." Since that described me, I found great comfort in knowing I was saved. It is still a great comfort today.

At Woodrow, I had to memorize an Edgar A. Guest poem that starts, "I have to live with myself, and so, I want to be fit for myself to know. I want to be able, as the days go by, always to look myself straight in the eye."

I never advanced beyond Tenderfoot, but the things I learned as a Boy Scout have always been touchstones. The Scout Oath: "On my honor I will do my best to do my duty to God and my Country, to obey the Scout Law, and to keep myself physically strong and mentally awake." The Scout Law: "A Scout is trustworthy, loyal, helpful, friendly, courteous, kind, obedient, cheerful, thrifty, brave, clean and reverent." Very high goals, but all attainable.

I was always a sort of a pacifist. In spite of teasing, some bullying, and being called "sissy" and "chicken," I was not convinced that physical confrontation was necessary. That attitude ended when I was fourteen.

I spent an entire morning in my room with my bike. I polished it, touched up the paint, greased the brake assembly, and oiled all the moving parts. It was beautiful! Like new! I rode it down to a small park and joined the guys in some game. Verlen, my main antagonist over the years, got on my pride and joy and started to ride off. I asked him to please not do that but my request was ignored. Our game was interrupted for a "water break." There was no fountain but one of the fellows had brought a wide mouth jar of water and we stood in line for a swig.

Just as it became my turn, Verlen returned with my treasure. I had the jar in my hand when he grabbed it, insisting it was his turn. I emptied the jar in his face and said, "You want it? You got it." He took a swing at me and hurt my ear. That was it. I turned loose on him and I can still feel the moisture of his eye on the back of my fist. He was shocked! I was furious. He was totally unprepared for such an onslaught and he had no time to mount an offense since he was trying to defend himself from this unknown demon. I continued to beat on him as he backed out of the park, across the street and ended up with this back against a bank with me still pounding.

Finally, some of the guys pulled me off and said, "Come on, Wiley, he's had enough." I was not particularly proud of my actions, but it was impressed on me that, yes, some things may be physically worth fighting for.

Age fourteen was memorable for another reason. Girls!

Especially that pretty, shy, blonde girl from Sunday school and the church choir. I learned her name was Maxine Anderson. She lived in a nice house at 1808 North Rustin.

It had indoor plumbing! Both of her parents had good jobs so she may have been a cut above the kid from Carlin Street. We talked some and became friends. Over time we became good friends. We always seemed to end up together at any Sunday school or church function.

When there was church on Sunday night, I learned that she always went down to Cookie's, the corner grocery, to get lunch meat for her school lunches. It was not a coincidence that I was always at the store to walk her home. It was on one of these walks that I got my first kiss. What a difference! We became more serious over the years and we were determined to get married. We would have a white house trimmed in green with a red gravel driveway. Since we were both only children we agreed to have at least two children. We walked together and rode bikes together.

Oddly, Maxine and I never did "date" date. I worked too hard for my money to spend it on a girl, even this special girl. I did, however, always manage to outbid other guys for the supper she prepared for box lunches at church. In high school things were difficult. Seniors, like me, seldom spoke to any sophomore in the hallway; not even the most beautiful of the bunch. We were always together at church, but strangers at school.

The summer of the year I was fourteen I got my first full time job and was on a payroll. The *Sioux City Tribune* opened a radio station, KTRI. I went to visit the studio when they had an open house. It was beautiful but all of the glass that enclosed the broadcast booths was smeared where kids had placed their hands and noses. I told the reception-ist my impressions. I did not know that she was the wife of the manager. She used the inner phone to call him out and when I told him that he should get someone to clean the glass he said, "Do you have any suggestions?"

I said, "Yes sir, me". He hired me on the spot and his wife helped me fill out the application for a Social Security number.

I cleaned the windows and continued to do "flunky" work around the studio. My main job was to get on my bike each hour and go down to the Tribune and pick up galley proofs of the newspaper and bring them back to the studio for the news broadcasts. The Sioux City Cowboys baseball team was a farm team of the Saint Louis Cardinals. When the team was in town, I had to accompany the print and broadcast reporters to the game. I was to run errands as they directed and fetch their cold drinks and snacks. This was great. I met the Concession Manager and long after I left KTRI I worked the grandstands at baseball and high school and semi-pro football games. I remember the chants: "Coke, cold drinks, cold pot." "Hot dogs. A loaf of bread, a pound of meat and all the mustard you can eat. Hot dogs." When summer was over and I could no longer work full time, the men in the press box welcomed me and I ran their errands for tips. On the way home after a game I passed the Dixie Cream Donut Shop. This was before automation and the baker rolled out the dough and cut the doughnuts by hand. Sometimes he would nick the side of one but that was not noticeable until it had been fried and glazed. These were ideal for an ever hungry young hustler for ten cents a dozen. During the bike ride home I would consume the whole dozen of those warm, tasty gems.

At fifteen things really began to pop. I could now have a regular paper route. That meant confirmed customers and a sure income. I did not have to do many sales, just delivery and collection. Normally we folded the paper into a six inch square and tossed it on the front porch. When I took over the route, I was told that one old woman wanted an unfolded paper placed on a table in the sun room at the back of the house. What a pain! But, and a big but, every Friday night the exact change and the card we punched as a receipt were on that sun room table. She never missed. I never had to make change. I learned that good service leads to good response.

I started high school. No transportation was provided. In later years I learned that a brisk walk was about four miles an hour. Since it took about an hour to walk to Central High, it must have been about four miles. It wasn't bad until the Iowa winter dipped to twenty below. But we had an answer to that, too. The dad of one of the guys was the engineer on a switch engine. About the time we were going to school, he was going down to the stock yards. A switch engine has a platform in front rather than a cow catcher. He would stop for us; we would get aboard and open our coats to face that big, hot boiler. It was heaven! There was one hitch. The engineer insisted that we not get on or off the platform while the engine was moving, even slightly. Banishment indefinitely was the punishment for misbehavior. It was a small price to pay for a warm ride from 18ᵗʰ to 11ᵗʰ Streets on a freezing morning.

With jobs as my priority, nearly all of my extra curricular activity was limited to school hours. I sang in the chorus and the a cappella choir. We combined to present an operetta once a year. In sophomore year anyone who could sing could join the chorus. As a junior or as senior, you had to audition for the music director. My heart was in my throat when I sang *The Lost Chord*. Fewer boys auditioned so it was easier for us than for the girls. I enjoyed this music very much, but the cherry on the sundae was when the choir made a trip to Sioux Falls, South Dakota, and visited George Washington High School. They had a top notch facility that was like a fancy theater.

While I was still a sophomore I came close to wearing myself out. I had done my paper route and made the Friday night collections. I had been accepted for a job working in the kitchen at the fancy Green Gables Restaurant. I rode my bike to the north side and started washing dishes, with a machine, and pots and pans, by hand, about six p.m.

The eight hour shift ended at two a.m. I got on my bike and rode farther north to my regular Saturday job at the Piggly Wiggly Market. I just slept at the door until the store opened at seven. I stocked shelves and boxed and carried out groceries until seven that evening. I rode my bike home and, believe me, it was very hard to get up and deliver the Sunday papers. I kept my Saturday job at Piggly Wiggly even when I was working during the week at the Dr. Pepper Bottling Plant, but spent no more eight hour shifts in a restaurant kitchen.

Our school paper, *The Record*, was published once a week. It was printed by students in the school print shop which was equipped with a linotype and presses. The students were mostly those that had tried printing in junior high. My junior year I was a reporter. We had a faculty advisor who explained copy form and the rules of journalism. This was great since my life long ambition had been to be a newspaper reporter. My senior year I was the sports editor and wrote a column called *Just Bob'n Around*.

One of the few major disappointments in my life came when I was a senior. I had been cast in the senior class play entitled *The Hottentot*. We had had one rehearsal when a friend called my mother and offered me a job after school and weekends at his downtown service station and parking lot. College was looming so the answer was clear. One of my classmates wrote in my yearbook, "Bob, we really missed you in the play."

If it is possible for a single event to change the direction of life years later, I think it was in Mr. Erickson's English class when I was a senior. We were to study Shakespeare and the first day of class he asked, "How many of you have studied The Bard before?" Nearly everyone raised a hand. "How many of you enjoyed it?" A couple of girls signified yes. He stated that this was about par for the course. Then he explained that these works were written, not to teach lessons in philosophy or morals, but to entertain. They were plays! Then he had us take out our books.

"Now read the stage directions," he ordered. Stage center, downstage right, upstage left. Then he assigned parts. "Now let's present a play." Wow! Words came alive! I wondered why more teachers weren't like this. On the spot, my thoughts of becoming a reporter were replaced. My college major became English-Speech. Little did I know that years later those words would appear on a military record and my life would change direction.

The weekend after I graduated, the whole gang from church had a picnic and swimming party at Brown's Lake, about ten miles south of town. I had never seen my girl in a swim suit. Wow! How she had blossomed! My buddy drove a Model A Ford coupe and Maxine and I cuddled in the rumble seat on the cool, breezy ride back to town. We parked in a seclude spot. My teen-aged hormones raged and with that warm, soft body next to me the last thing on my mind was the commandment prohibition against what was about to happen.

But at the first clumsy pass, she pushed my hand away and said, "Bob Wiley, I love you because you are a nice guy, but if you quit being a nice guy, I won't have anything to do with you." I didn't understand. I was confused. I was frustrated. I was furious! I got out of the rumble seat and stormed home, vowing to never speak to her again. For the few months until I left for college, I avoided her and if we ended up in the same room, I ignored her. It was over!

My first job out of high school was at the Cudahy Packing Plant. At seventy cents an hour, and a dollar five an hour for overtime, I was rolling in dough! Money to spend and the college fund account at the Troy National Bank grew.

My first assignment was in the hog coolers. I wore a white coat, a canvas cap and white cotton gloves. It was my job to get the hogs as they came from the kill and move them to the coolers. The carcasses were hung by their back legs from an overhead device on a track. Since they weighed much more than I did, I could only move them by putting my head on the backbone through the open body cavity, hook my arms at the elbows over the two front legs and push. With my grease-soaked cotton gloves, I had the softest, whitest hands you ever saw.

Then I was transferred to the beef cut to become what they called a "cowboy." The beef coolers were on the floor above us. There was a grease covered chute with sides that went from a hole in the floor of the beef coolers down to a table about four feet wide where there were three butchers on each side. Each had a short, thin, sharp boning knife used to remove all the meat from the bones. The meat was put in stainless steel barrels to be taken to the processing division to make wieners and lunch meats. The bones were put in like barrels and taken to the rendering plant.

It was my job to stop the beef quarters that were dropped from the floor above so that they did not slam into the butchers with their flashing knives. The quarters weighed between 150 and 250 pounds and when they hit the bottom they had acquired considerable speed. When I threw my two meat hooks into them, it liked to pull my arms out of their sockets and snap my head into the next block. But it was my job and I persisted.

I had worked about an hour when old Pollack barked, "G-damn it, tell the kid." One of the men came over and took my meat hooks. When the next carcass came down, it jerked him as it had me. Instead of moving the meat to the table, he pushed it back up into the chute and wedged it in the sides. When the next piece came down, he just held the first one in the chute and it took the fierce impact. Lesson: I am sure that had I complained, nobody would have said a word. Just shut up and do the job and everything will work out for the better.

Another lesson I learned on my own. The hottest, stinkiest part of the entire plant was the rendering plant. Several times an hour I had to take barrels of bones there. I soon learned that standing outside the door, taking a big breath and holding it; I could rush in, dump my load and rush out. And I could do so without having to take a breath or inhaling the smell.

After working about a month or six weeks, the foreman came to me and asked, "Wiley, how old are you?"

"I was born in 1924".

"Don't be a smart ass. How old are you?"

"I am seventeen, but I will be eighteen in September."

"I'm sorry, kid. You are a good worker, but our insurance

will not let us hire anyone under eighteen." So ended the gravy train.

I heard there was work at Sue Bee Honey. I was hired on the spot as was an old friend from junior high. Our job? To move half a railroad coal car full of coal to the coal bin in the basement. It was hard enough throwing shovels full of coal over the side of the car and onto the chute. The real work was down in the basement moving coal from the bottom of the chute and spreading it out over the bin. We did it in two days, but Frank quit. I got moved to one of the machines that filled the jars with honey. Across from me worked Bonnie, a real doll. Nothing came of that even though Maxine and I were estranged.

When I returned to Sioux City for my twenty-five year high school reunion, I visited the factory and told the manager about the machine I used to operate. His response was, "Oh, yes. We have that machine in the basement. We are going to put it in our museum." Talk about being brought back to reality!

When September rolled around, I was off to Iowa State Teachers College in Cedar Falls, Iowa. When I stepped off the bus, I had arranged for a job in the student union for my meals and I had cash in my pocket for my tuition, books and fees, and my first semester rent in Seeley Hall. I signed up for sixteen credit hours and soon had a part-time job as a janitor to start saving for my second semester costs. My student union work was in the kitchen and serving in the cafeteria food line. I met lots of girls on that line. But the more I saw of them, the more I thought of what I had had back home. Maxine was the kind of girl that I wanted to marry. If that was to be the case, I thought she had a right to expect the same from me. I made a promise to myself which I have kept. In spite of temptations, opportunities, passes, offers, close calls and provocations, I have never committed adultery. I don't know how much of that can be attributed to remembering the commandment or how much was because of my love and respect for my girl who became my wife.When I hitchhiked home for Thanksgiving, I apologized for my prior behavior, the apology was accepted and we continued to discuss future plans. I returned to school a happier person.

Between jobs and classes, I found time to be a cheerleader. Not that I was so good, but few guys were willing to do it.

The student union gig got better too. I was assigned to the soda fountain. And every future teacher was required to pass a written and practical etiquette test, which I had done, and was required to learn to dance. I never had time to learn in high school so this was my chance. I took lessons and passed the course, but I was not very good. That's where the soda fountain fit in. It was located just across the hall from the dance hall. There was a record player there and when there was a lull in business, there were a number of girls who were more than willing to help me progress. We could dance and I could keep my eye open for business. The best of both worlds.

The reconciliation with Maxine continued while I was home for Christmas. Plans for marriage became more serious. She was more eager than I since I was unsure what the future held for me. I returned to school.

I got a major break about the end of the semester. I got a forty hour a week job as a billing clerk for the Rath Packing Company in Waterloo, the city just across the Cedar River from Cedar Falls. I could give up my student union and janitorial jobs and just pay for things. The hardest part was paying for meals. We arranged our classes so that after the last one, about 3p.m., we could catch the interurban street car that went right to the plant. We would do our homework en route. We would work from four to midnight, Monday through Thursday. Since some games and dances were normally held on Friday nights, the company had us work from midnight until eight Saturday morning. That was good except for one time. When I got back to the dorm, I put on my cheerleader sweater and thought I would take a nap until game time. How can I forget sleeping through the first three quarters of the homecoming game?

As soon as I turned eighteen and signed up for the draft, I went to a Navy recruiting office to get into Naval Aviation. I had always been impressed by the flyers white uniforms and fancy planes in the movies. I passed the written test and went for the physical. Everything went okay until they asked if I had ever had any problems. When he got to hay fever I said, "Yes," and the doctor said I was disqualified. I asked how much ragweed was in the middle of the ocean, but it didn't change the answer.

I was both disappointed and angry. I figured they would have to come and get me. Never again would I ever admit to suffering from hay fever as a kid. They did come and get me. My notice said I was to report for duty May 14. What? A month before finals? I went to the dean of men and pleaded my case. Was it fair for me to get all "incompletes" after working so hard all semester? He agreed that he would allow any grade that my professors would agree to. All were fair except one S.O.B. of a history prof. I had told him I did not have time while working forty hours and carrying sixteen credit hours to give him a book report each week. I passed every test and quiz with flying colors, but he gave me a "D." To this day I think that was unfair

The brief break between college and service was not a happy time. Maxine and I were both pretty broken up, not knowing when we would be together again. That last embrace was tearful on both sides. But I had to do what needed to be done. I had to become a man.

Greetings, You're Drafted

"Greetings from the President of the United States."
Really? A personal letter to me? Don't you believe it. This
was the salutation on the letter to all Selective Service draftees informing them of the date and place to they were required to report for duty. My date was May 14, 1943. The
place was Camp Douglas outside Des Moines, Iowa. Oddly
enough, that was the same camp my father was discharged
from following World War I.

Many draftees were less than enthusiastic about being in
the service. That was not the case with me. It could not have
been better. I had plenty to eat and a place to sleep. "Three
hots and a cot." They gave me clothes and did my laundry
and dry cleaning. I could get my personal items from the
post exchange at a reduced price and pay only a quarter to
see a movie at the post theater. And on the top of all that,
they paid me fifty dollars a month! I bought an eighteen
dollar plus war bond every month, had money to spend,
and could even send some money back to the little Glendale

Baptist Church to help buy a little electric organ. This life was going to be great! Challenging and full of possible danger, but great!

Upon arrival at Camp Douglas, we were given a complete physical and numerous shots. Then we were given a couple of bags to carry our belongings. We were issued uniforms and for the first in my life I knew that I wore a size 10½ D boot. We shipped our civilian clothes home, were indoctrinated and issued a serial number. We were informed that to pick up our food tray for supper we must be able to give our name and serial number. "Wiley, 37670849." I got supper.

The Army does not allow for much just standing around. Along the main road there were three foot high, six inch posts, painted white. Quite attractive. A non-commissioned officer showed a group of us privates the marks where additional posts were to be installed. A truck came around and dropped off posthole diggers, shovels and posts. Six foot posts! For a three foot fence! Mr. Posthole Digger fast became an enemy.

Not long after, we were herded onto a train and informed that we were headed for Camp Joseph T. Robinson at Little Rock, Arkansas, the Medical Corps basic training facility. A medic! Sit in a dispensary, give shots and keep records. What a deal!

The first thing I did was to have my bleeding ingrown toe nail taken care of. It took only a minute and hurt like sin. The relief was worth it.

At our first inspection the first sergeant asked, "Soldier, do you shave?"

"No, sir."

"Get a razor and start. And don't call me 'sir.' That is for officers. Call me sergeant!"

Lesson one.

We did calisthenics and did close order drill. We learned Army organization: squad, platoon, company, battalion and up. Our company commander was a major from the south who pronounced "ambulance" as "am-a-lance." We did calisthenics and close order drill. We learned medical terms and how to take a pulse. We did calisthenics and close order drill. I learned to drill so well that I became a "lance" corporal. That meant I wore a band on my arm. The band had corporal stripes. I was uniquely qualified for this position. I could tell my left from my right, I had a loud voice and I could count to four. "Hut, two, three, four."

As a "lance" corporal I could not be as mean as the real corporal who was our squad leader. He was a little pipsqueak who thought his authority came directly from God. If some GI turned left when the command was right, the tyrant would yell for a minute and a half. He was the meanest human I ever met.

At about this time I learned a valuable lesson that stayed with me throughout my military career. The first sergeant asked for four volunteers to do some easy task. I thought if I did my part it would be over and done with. Then when the nasty, dirty jobs came up I would be safe since I had done my part. I raised my hand and gave the sergeant my name. BIG mistake! From then on whenever any task required man power it was "Wiley, and you, and you." Never again!

We learned the various types of wounds and injuries. I learned that the compound fracture of a bone did not mean that it was broken in several places, but that the bone punctured the skin. We learned to properly bandage various parts of the body.

As I walked my half mile this morning and my legs began to ache, I thought of the thirty mile jaunts we took in basic. We ran the infantry basic training obstacle course located on the other side of the base. It was full of walls, ropes, fences and ditches.

Then we would come back and run the medic course. On this one I carried a man on a litter. The only thing harder than trying to dig a foxhole in the Arkansas shale while lying on your side, is trying to push a litter loaded with a 150 pound "patient" under a barbed wire fence or up a fifteen degree incline.

I wondered what all this had to do with giving shots in a dispensary. I asked Lt. Murphy, our platoon commander, what they were training us for. He said, "You are to be an aid man assigned to an infantry company and where they go, you go."

I then asked when we were going to get our small arms training. "Oh no," he said, "You will just have a red cross on your helmet to identify you as a medic.

The idea of being shot at with no chance to retaliate did

not appeal to me so I asked, "How do you get out of this outfit?" When he said there was no way, I was needed here; this brash private shot back, "Sir, I don't believe that!"

Murphy was surprised. Draftees did not speak to officers like that. Fortunately for me, he just smiled and said, "Well, I'll check." There was nothing to do but wait.

One night I was on my cot and was called to the orderly room (headquarters) for a phone call from Sioux City. What could be bad wrong? The female voice on the phone said, "Hi, dear, it's me, Maxine."

"What's wrong? What's the trouble?"

Calmly, she said, "Nothing's wrong. I just wanted to call and say I love you and I miss you."

Great! I was bone tired. I had been awakened from a restful sleep. I was very upset, but she loved me! How could I be upset? We talked and I assured her that I loved her too, I was well and healthy, and that I would try to write more often.

Lt. Murphy returned and told me I did have some options. I could apply to go to air crew training. I could try for OCS, Officer Candidate School. Or there was an Army Specialized Training Program, ASTP, where I could learn a specialty like dental technician, office manager or bookkeeper - all skills that could be used in civilian life. As a last resort, I could ask for a transfer to the paratroopers. I went back to my cot to ponder.

I thought about the options. Officers made more money than enlisted men. Flying officers made more than ground officers. ASTP could help when I was discharged. I applied for, was accepted and passed the physical for Air Crew Training. No more red cross on the helmet!

When my buddies shipped out I was retained as permanent party because of the change I made. There was no job slot for me and I was relegated to KP and guard duty. KP or kitchen police, was an eight to twelve hour shift peeling potatoes, preparing vegetables and washing dishes, pots and pans. Guard duty was just walking around the post sewage disposal pond with a night stick. I must have done a good job since no spy tried to break in and the pond did not escape. That was it, each of the duties on alternate days.

There was one bright spot. On guard I had lots of time to think, mostly about the girl I left behind. One of her cousins one time called her Maxie which I edited to Mickey. The nickname stuck with all of our acquaintances and our entire married life.

Finally my orders came through. I was sent to Sheppard Field at Wichita Falls, Texas. Here I joined GI's from other branches that had transferred to the Air Corps from infantry, artillery, engineers, and from the medics. All had been through basic training and some had been in the service for some time. A few were even non-commissioned officers. Our experience would later give us an advantage over those aviation cadets that entered the program directly from civilian life.

Life at Sheppard was mostly calisthenics and close order drill. The worst part was the water. Even on a hot, dusty,

West Texas drill field, I could not stand to drink the water. It was only in the mess hall when the water was cold, that I could manage to drink it.

When the Army had assembled one hundred of us, we were designated Aviation Cadets and were shipped to the College Training Detachment (CTD) at Montana State College at Bozeman. It was only early fall but we were issued our winter gear almost immediately. That gave us our first clue as to the severity of Montana winters. We were to be stationed there for six months. With six squadrons, a new unit would arrive each month and one would depart. We slept in a new dormitory with real beds which was a most welcome change. To the best of my knowledge, there were no male students, but between the female students and Army nurses there were plenty of females around. Too bad we didn't have more time off! Our studies included physics and trigonometry, a far cry from the dreaded algebra and plane geometry of Woodrow Wilson Junior High School. But there was a welcome break.

We got orientation rides in a two-seater Piper Cub. The grizzled old instructor did something interesting before we flew. He explained that some of us may suffer from motion fright or "air sickness." He said that was the normal body reaction to unnatural conditions or emotions. He called it nature's "fight or flee" reaction. He compared it to a wild horse in a corral for the first time. A horse would be frightened and uncertain so it would raise its tail and rid itself of bodily waste so it is more prepared to fight or flee.

Fortunately, on my first flight I did not have this symptom.

When the engine started there was no reaction like that of the frightened three-year-old back in Wiggins. This was way cool! We took off and at altitude my instructor explained and then demonstrated a stall and a spin. Oddly enough, even the spin did not frighten me. Then he let me handle the controls. After a while he took back the controls and taught me a lesson that I still practice. He told me to take my hands and feet off the controls. Then he put the plane in a slight nose high altitude and released the controls! The Cub drifted slowly off to the side and started down. As it gained speed, it righted itself and started another slow climb. With nobody on the controls, it repeated this slight dive-slight climb pattern for a few minutes. Finally the old timer resumed control and said, "See, the plane knows HOW to fly, you just tell it WHERE to fly. If you find yourself gripping the controls, relax and treat them gently, just as you would a girl."

Ever since I entered basic training, Mickey and I had corresponded regularly. We talked about our daily lives and our plans for the future. Each time the subject of marriage came up; there was the same difference of opinion. She kept asking that we do something immediately and I insisted that we should wait until or if, I got home and see what my physical condition might be. I did not want to leave her a widow or possibly with a child without a father.

One day I got a letter again outlining all the reasons why this was the time. It ended with, "Sweetheart, it is now or never!" An ultimatum? That upset me to the point that I did what could have become the biggest disaster of my young life. I got a penny postcard, put her name and address on it, turned it over and printed in large letters "N-E-V-E-R." Did this end our plans? Only time would tell.

CTD was tough, but there were certain advantages. There was no close order drill, but we did have a "retreat" parade six evenings a week. Each event was judged and the winning squadron did not have to stay in the dorm and study, but was allowed to go to the student union where there were girls! I soon concluded that the student nurses were considerably more "worldly" than regular female students.

I made friends with the daughter of a Montana rancher. Her name, oddly enough, was Mickey. Although it was no longer technically true, I told her at the onset that there could be nothing serious because I had a girl back home I planned to marry. We danced, we cuddled, we took long walks in the snow and even borrowed a kids' sled to make some runs down a hill in the park. We went out to dinner on the weekends and I spent time in her sorority house. When it came time for me to ship out, it was a very tearful farewell. Even though I had told her from the start that there could be nothing serious, she asked if I knew for sure that I would not return. I assured her that was the case and suggested that she find a nice 4F (unqualified for military service) boy and marry him. Was she convinced? Again, only time would tell.

With the frigid Montana winter, the Army made sure

that we were issued warm clothing. We were given heavy wool overcoats that reached almost to mid-calf. We had fur lined flight boots that were nearly tall enough to reach the bottom of the overcoat. For some of the shorter guys, the two did meet. It lead to a memorable situation.

The recorded bugle call sounded reveille at 6 a.m. Assembly was sounded at 6:30. Most men in the squadron climbed out of the sack at reveille to shave, shower and dress. A minority loved sleep so they stayed in bed until assembly and only then did they don cap, gloves, overcoats and boots. After all flights had reported, the cadet sergeant turned to Lt. Franklin, saluted, and announced, "All present or accounted for, sir."

The lieutenant returned the salute and ordered, "Sergeant, have the men remove their coats!"

"Sir?" was all the shocked sergeant could say.

Franklin repeated the order.

"Yes sir." He faced the troops and said, "By the numbers, remove coats. One, unbutton coats. Two, remove coats." He turned and reported that the order had been complied with.

There stood about a quarter of the squadron in the Montana cold with nothing but hat, gloves, boots and underwear. In about fifteen or twenty seconds Lt. Franklin ordered, "Sergeant, dismiss the squadron." Nothing more was said. No names were taken. No demerits were issued. The culprits learned not to report undressed. I learned that officers accomplished a lot without punishment. I never forgot that.

Our six months at Montana State ended and we were shipped to the Classification Center at Santa Anna, California. We were joined by one hundred cadets from another CTD and designated Squadron 83. That number would have an impact in the future.

We took more mental and physical dexterity tests than I ever knew existed. There was very little marching except for the Sunday parades. Physical training was another matter. We had an hour each morning and another hour each afternoon. Then there was the occasional half mile run. When we first arrived, we had taken what was called a physical fitness test or PRT. It consisted of three phases; pull-ups on an overhead bar, sit ups and a fifty yard run over a ten yard course.

Soon after completing the test, we were awarded a plaque showing that we scored higher than any other incoming class. This may have been due to our conditioning before entering the aviation cadet program. When the plaque was presented we learned that there was also recognition for the unit that showed the greatest improvement. Someone came up with an idea. Each fitness phase had a certain criteria which scored one hundred percent. We were Squadron 83. Why not set a goal of eighty-three percent for our final test? Some guys, including me, had trouble with the overhand pull-ups. Others were somewhat slow afoot. But everyone, with working out, should be able to do 116 sit ups for a one hundred percent score. Every spare minute, some buddy would hold my feet and I would do as many as

I could. Gradually, I built up the repetitions. To my amazement, I got to the 116 mark. In a perfect world, I would be writing that the squadron scored eighty-three percent, but it was not to be. Every man in the squadron did 116 sit ups, and we did win the plaque for "most improved," but we fell short of our goal by about one and a half percent.

We also had other training. On the firing range we became familiar with the 45 caliber pistol, the carbine, and the Thompson Sub Machine Gun. We learned to "field strip" the weapons which means to dismantle them completely and reassemble. I was fairly competent when firing the carbine, but I was less than average with the other two.

I learned not to judge others when it came to aquatic training. We went down to a Pacific beach, lined up four abreast, and were instructed to run to the water, swim under the water as far as we could, then surface and swim around the pier. Clear enough. But as each foursome hit the water, they would surface immediately. Were they stupid? Did they not understand? Did they know what swim under water meant? When I ran to the water and dove in I understood! That water was so cold it took your breath away. My body made me surface immediately. Don't judge others! Who would have thought that on a warm, sunny Southern California winter afternoon that the Pacific could be so icy?

Finally, the day of reckoning arrived and I was ecstatic. A friend who worked in the headquarters had seen the test results and I was qualified for training in all three areas: pilot, navigator and bombardier. The graduating class assembled in the auditorium. In the front of the room there was an officer at each of three tables marked pilot, navigator and bombardier. The officers called out names and the cadets went forward to receive their orders. My ears were attuned to the pilot desk. Suddenly I was aware of the officer at the navigator table, clearly upset shouting, "Wiley, Robert B."

I walked up, saluted and said, "Sir, there must be some mistake. I am qualified as a pilot." He said I had been assigned to navigation school and pointed out a place for me to sign. I said, "Sir, do I have to accept this?"

He snapped, "Hell no you don't have to sign. You can go back to the Infantry!" I signed.

In a few days, some of us, including my buddy Jens, were on our way to the navigation school at Hondo, Texas, about thirty miles west of San Antonio. It was hot, dusty and generally unattractive. The wooden barracks were a far cry from the beautiful dorms at Montana State.

There were three basic forms of navigation. Celestial determined location relative to a fixed heavenly body.

Dead reckoning used heading, indicated air speed and wind to plot course. Pilotage was a visual comparison of surroundings to what was on a map. We had to learn all three and it was hard! Between the heat, the study, the marching and the calisthenics, I was very down. That continued until one day I sat on my bunk and vowed, "These bastards can't make it hard enough for me to quit!" But I came close.

We were on a visual flight over the hot, bleak wasteland of West Texas. The turbulence was horrific. I became air sick beyond all belief. I upchucked into a handy vessel. The instructor came back and asked, "Wiley, where are we?"

"I don't know."

"Do you want to wash out?"

"I don't care."

Fortunately he was sympathetic and I survived, physically and career-wise.

We had to memorize celestial constellations, remember the various types of maps and use E6B handheld, manual computers, and sextants to shoot the stars. After what seemed like an eternity, the training was finished and I pinned on the silver wings and the coveted gold bars of a second lieutenant.

We were given our new orders, but were granted a thirty day leave. Four of us went to Union Station in San Antonio to get a train to the Pacific Northwest. Jens was from a small town outside Tacoma and my mother was working at a DuPont nuclear plant at Hanford, Washington. I can't remember the other guys.

"Sorry, there are no seats available." We were crushed. Here we were starting our leaves, with nothing to do. We were helpless. "Unless you are willing to share a compartment." Halleluiah! We grabbed it. As it turned out splitting the cost four ways was actually cheaper than coach fare.

When we went through Utah, the train filled with college girls who were headed back to school. They were duly impressed with these young men in uniform with the silver wings. We did not need the wings to float through the rest of the trip.

The leave was over and we reported to the Combat Crew Assignment Center in Lemoore, California. I was assigned to a crew that had a pilot from Mississippi, a co-pilot from Iowa, and a bombardier from Massachusetts. The six enlisted men on the crew were from New Jersey and Georgia to Wyoming and Nebraska. The co-pilot, Pappy, was twenty-nine, the engineer and the tail gunner were each twenty-two. Even with those three, the average age on the ten person crew was just under twenty! We were kids about to become men.

We were shipped to the Combat Crew Training Center at Walla Walla, Washington. We were assigned a brand new B-24 Liberator bomber. Coming from the little six passenger plane I had flown in navigation school, it seemed gigantic! My navigator table sat behind the pilot and across the walkway from the radio operator. I had to become familiar with the gun positions, turrets and handheld. When it came time for me to get into the ball turret, or belly gun, the crew had to stand on the hatch to compress my six-foot-frame into a space sized for a large midget. When I got excited during a fighter pass I moved my controls too quickly and they spun me like a top.

We had a lot of training and indoctrination, but during our off duty time we managed to date girls from Whitman College. Jens' crew and mine were close. He and I double dated. My date, Dolly, smoked. Since the military could get cigarettes and the girls could not, the only gentlemanly thing to do was to give her a carton of cigarettes. Bad move. We would go out and she would say, "Bob, I don't have a purse. Would you carry the pack?" Then it became "Will you light one for me?" You can guess the rest. For the first time since I made the promise to my mother, I began to smoke. That habit continued until I was about 45 and quit "cold turkey" to spend the most miserable six months of my life in withdrawal.

Dating did have one good result. Although under age, bars served men in uniform "as their patriotic duty." My mother had always preached, "If you would not become a drunkard you must never drink a drop. If you never do begin you will never have to stop." I really had never given it much thought. During the time at Walla Walla, I must have tried every alcoholic beverage made by man. Mixed, straight or on the rocks I hated it all! Not even beer. Right then I thought why should I do something that I hate, and which costs so much, just to fit in and be accepted? It made no sense. I am still a teetotaler, have no objection to others drinking and my friends accept me as I am.

During training there were missions for every crew position. There was formation flying, bombing, gunnery and navigation. There was one hitch. For my celestial mission, the pilot decided to go "sight seeing." My training was shot and I just followed the course he flew. His folly would later cause him some anxiety.

With our training completed, we flew our new bird to a base called, as I recall, Fairfield-Suisun outside Sacramento,

California. We had little to do except run fuel consumption test flights to the Oregon border and back.

During our off time, we officers went to town. One day, we located an ice rink. The two guys from Iowa and the one from Massachusetts all knew how to skate, but it took some persuasion to get the Mississippi pilot onto the ice. Finally we convinced him. The bombardier and I each took an arm and took him around the rink. We started slowly but went faster and faster. The rebel kept insisting, "Let me go. Let me go."

We got on the straightaway and I said, "Okay let him." We did and he sailed to the end of the rink, doubled over when he hit the short end wall, and groped his way back to the dressing area, clinging to the wall for dear life.

At a USO dance, I met a girl named JoAnn. We became quite friendly and she and her parents invited me to join them for Christmas dinner. I was to meet them at the USO Christmas Day. Then, disaster! On December 22 we were restricted to the base pending overseas departure. No phone calls. No letters. Nothing. Complete isolation. We left Christmas Eve!

The Pacific Theater of Operations

While we were in Sacramento the other crew members chipped in and purchased twenty cases of Canadian whiskey. The liquor, along with our equipment and personal belongings had already been loaded on our B-24, and at thirteen minutes after midnight we took off headed for Hawaii. After we left the shore lights of California, the night became very dark especially for an apprehensive young second lieutenant navigator. No landmarks. No radios. No radar. Only my instruments, manuals and a sky full of millions of stars. And I had not done any celestial missions since I left Hondo in what seemed like an eternity ago. I wondered if the pilot regretted not letting me do my job at Walla Walla.

I plotted fix after fix and we stayed right on course. All night long the queries came: "Gunner to Navigator. How are we doing sir?"

"Engineer to Navigator. How are we doing, sir?"

The pilot asked, "Bob are we okay?" Each time I assured

them, I became more confident in my ability. Then, panic! My last fix showed us thirty miles off course. But that was only half the problem. It was getting toward daylight and the dim sky made it impossible to see the stars. The sun had not yet come up so I could not shoot a "sun line." Fortunately the crew had come to believe in me and there were no more "how are we doings?" My next fix showed us back on course. The only harm was to my ego. I had screwed up. I was not perfect. We landed at John Rogers Field at 1:13 PM, 1313 hours, military time.

We had an unforgettable Christmas dinner of hot dogs and fresh pineapple juice. The pilot had opened our sealed orders and he told the crew we had been assigned to the 13th Air Force in the SWPA, the Southwest Pacific Area. We left the next morning, headed south to Canton Island, Tarawa and Guadalcanal.

We had always landed on paved or smooth coral runways. At "Canal" we thought our plane was coming apart. The runway was of pierced steel plank, a series of four foot by eight foot steel pieces that rattled when we landed. The noise was nerve wracking.

After a brief stay, we flew to Nadzab, a staging base on the Eastern end of New Guinea. Following some orientation, we flew two bombing missions to Wewak, a Japanese supply base that had been bypassed by American ground forces as they island hopped north. When we continued to Beak, on the western end of New Guinea, we met our first disappointment as a crew. They took away our plane! We had tested it, babied it and become very fond of our new bird. Now it was gone. Dejected, we off loaded our things, along with the twenty cases from Canada, loaded it all on a C-46 and headed for Morotai, the base of operations for our combat tour. Our island home was about half way between New Guinea and the southern tip of the Philippines.

We were assigned a tent that had a wooden floor thanks to the previous occupants and the Navy Construction Battalion, "Sea Bees" stationed on the island. The bed was a two by four frame with aircraft tire inner tubes stretched between the sides. It was really quite comfortable. Our shower facility would have made the most avid environmentalist proud. About nine feet over the concrete floor was a wooden framework that supported about thirty fifty-five gallon steel barrels. Each morning, the barrels were filled with water and during the day the tropical sun would beat down on the setup. At 4 p.m. the crews would come in, wet down in about five seconds, turn off the water, wash with soap, and rinse off in another five seconds. I don't think any crew member used more than two quarts of water.

After a brief orientation, I was sent to navigator school. Why? We were now in the Southern Hemisphere with a whole new set of celestial bodies to learn. There was no North Star. It was replaced by the Southern Cross. There were no highways or railroads to follow. There were no radio beams with one exception; Long Range Air Navigation, LORAN, which used aircraft equipment to measure radio signals broadcast simultaneously from two different stations.

It worked perfectly on the <u>ground</u> but when a plane became airborne the humid air cooled, condensed, and shorted out the unit's electrical components. In short, it was useless.

I was also taught to make drift meter readings using the white caps on the waves. We could also determine surface winds by reading those whitecaps. When a whitecap breaks, it slides INTO the prevailing wind. The spray from the whitecap shows the wind velocity. No spray, the wind is calm. Heavy spray, the wind is over thirty-five knots. I don't remember all the intermediate steps. A "knot" is a nautical mile per hour.

Believe it or not, one can obtain a fix by shooting clouds! Ocean water heats very slowly. Not so with land masses including islands. If a navigator spots a thunderhead building on the horizon, he knows that there is a land mass, probably an island, at its base. Since he knows his approximate position, he looks on his map for an island near the location of the thunderhead. If there is more than one storm on the horizon, he takes reading on the center of each cloud, and where the lines from the clouds cross, that is his approximate position. Not much like using a GPS!

In retrospect I can say that with very few exceptions, my crew and I had a relatively safe combat tour. We did not face the dangers the Marines did in their island invasions. We were never threatened by a Japanese suicide bomber. We did not shiver in a frozen fox hole or march for days on muddy roads. Unlike our fellow airmen in the European Theater, we were not under constant attack by fighters and flak for virtually an entire mission. We were very fortunate in our assignment and I am truly grateful and feel blessed.

On our very first mission from Morotai, we had an engine quit when we were halfway to the target. We hoped that this was not an indicator of things to come. Fortunately, such an event did not reoccur during any of our remaining missions. Sometimes we flew as a single aircraft. Other times we flew in six, nine or eighteen ship formations. We hit numerous enemy held cities in the Philippines. Incidentally, I learned recently that after the war my pastor was a Lutheran missionary in Cebu City which was one of our targets.

For a while, day after day, we flew sea searches. We were to intercept and destroy all cargo ships which could carry supplies to enemy forces or to Japan itself. On one occasion six crews from our squadron were dispatched to patrol a 60,000 square mile area of the Celebes Sea. Each crew was responsible for a specific 10,000 square mile area. About four hours into the mission, the lead crew leader radioed that he had spotted a target ship and ordered us to rendezvous at his position.

My crew was the last to arrive. We were just in time to see the first bombing run. The ship was turning and the bombs missed. The ship sailed straight away. The second bomber started its run and, once again, the target turned and increased speed. Another miss!

Willie, our bombardier, and I guessed that the wily ship's captain was using binoculars to spot the bombs being released. Only then would he accelerate and turn. There was a third miss. Then we made an observation. We agreed that the ship had established a pattern. He alternated the direction of his evasive turns. First left, then right, then left again. As the most junior and least experienced crew, our pilot agreed that we should keep our mouths shut and not share our guess with the others. As we watched, bombers four and five missed. If our assumption was correct, the ship's next turn would be to the left. Since I figured that Bill knew how long it took the bombs to reach the water, I asked him if he could estimate the location of the ship from that time. He did some quick calculations and said, "I think so".

We started our bomb run. At "bombs away" the ship started to move left. Halleluiah! He let me look in the bomb sight and there was nothing in the cross hairs. Just as the ship's bow started to appear, Bill pushed me away and started to chant, "Hit. Hit. Hit, damn it hit."

At first nothing happened. Then the first bomb hit just astern. All the rest of the string marched up the center of the ship. When the smoke cleared, the two sides of the ship were lying flat in the water beside the sunken hull. Our crew bombardier was a cotton pickin' genius!

We had been on the island about two or three months when I got a letter that was forwarded from Bozeman, Montana. It was from "Montana Mickey." A young man had asked her to marry him and she wanted to be assured that I did not plan to return. At first I almost laughed. Then it about broke my heart. That poor, sweet, young girl had not believed me when I told her that I would not return and that I was going to marry the girl back in Iowa. I wrote a sincere letter of congratulations and best wishes. I also apologized for the delay in responding since I had just received her letter. I told her I hoped the delay had not caused her any problems.

That letter also had a profound effect on me. I had not really thought of my Mickey in quite some time. Then it became a most disconcerting daily thought.

Normally we flew only every second or third day which left us with a lot of free time. We played pool and shot craps at the Officer's Club. Before long I learned the odds on every throw of the dice. I was never very good but I did learn all the jargon. A "10" was "Big Dick from Boston bought him an Austin, there was room for his ass and a gallon of gas, but his balls hung out and he lost 'em."

There was lots of drinking at the club. A good day or a bad day was a reason to get drunk. And to me, it was all a pain. Time after time I was asked to join in. When I declined I was ridiculed as a "party pooper" or accused as someone who thought he was above the crowd. Finally in a combination of anger and frustration, I agreed that when our missions were over and our replacement crews arrived, I would get drunk with them. I would come to regret that capitulation.

We played softball and tag football. We swam and ran our outboard motor boat that was built of two discarded fuel tanks and an auxiliary power unit from an aircraft. And we played cards, lots of cards, including poker. I became a better than average poker player, but spent a fortune learning. We also enjoyed movies. That is, if you define enjoy as sitting on a bench in a steady rain, wrapped in a poncho, with an African pith helmet to keep your head dry. Nah, it wasn't bad. Bob Hope, Bing Crosby, and, especially, Dorothy Lamour, made it all worthwhile.

One other benefit of down time was that it gave us an opportunity to negotiate and celebrate. Following every mission we flew, tough or not, each crew member was given two ounces of whiskey. Some consumed it immediately. The four officers on my crew chose a different option. We each poured our ration into an empty fifth liquor bottle. Everything went in; scotch, bourbon, blend, brandy, domestic or import. It was an insult to a gourmet, but to the Navy Sea Bees on the island this was treated as one would a vintage bottle of champagne. The Navy frowned on the use of alcohol. With the correct approach, some sailor would be happy to exchange a Number 10 can of ice cream mix and a fifty pound box of steaks for the concoction that we had bottled. What a deal! Cooks in the mess hall were more than willing to do the preparation if they shared in the celebration. There was plenty for them, the ten members of our crew and invited members of other crews. How about the big wigs in the "head shed?" Don't be silly.

We continued to pound targets in the Philippines but in the back of our minds was always Balikpapan, without a doubt the most dangerous target we would ever face. It was an oil refinery and storage complex on the east coast

of Borneo. It was the most vital source for Japanese petro-
leum products in our area and it was defended accordingly.
We were told that months earlier our unit had suffered severe losses in repeated attempts to shut it down. After our
group's repeated strikes, the anti-aircraft flak forces had
been reduced from heavy to moderate. Somehow that was
not very comforting. We were now scheduled for the first of
what would be seven sorties against this target.

On the way I gave very little thought to the danger. I was
too busy doing my job. That changed when we arrived at the
I.P., the initial point at which the bomb run starts. I left my
navigator's table and assumed my strike duties. I sat on my
flak jacket on the floor just forward of the bomb bay. When
the bomb doors opened, I continually pushed on an auxiliary handle which kept the bomb bay doors from creeping
shut and closing off electrical current to the bomb racks. It
is hard to explain my emotions as I looked down at the black
puffs of smoke from the exploding flak and listened to the
pieces of shrapnel that rattled off our plane. It was not fear,
but it was more than apprehension. When the run was over
and the formation wheeled around and got back over the
water, the emotion was a mixture of relief and exhilaration.
One down and six to go!

Ever since I had received that letter from Montana, I
spent more and more time thinking about my Mickey. Had
I completely blown it with my NEVER? Was there still a
chance? Now was not the time to do anything about it, but
that did not stop me from thinking. I even made a "Marriage-

Ability" chart. Down the left side I wrote her name and the names of every girl I had ever dated. Across the top I wrote all the evaluation points. Everything was evaluated: looks, figure, legs, skin tone, height, intelligence, sense of humor, everything. I even included the width of the pelvic area since it could have a bearing on the ability to have children.

Each candidate was given a plus or a minus or a zero if I couldn't remember. When the chart was completed, the only girl that had a plus in every square was my Mickey. I was amazed. When I showed the remarkable chart to Pappy, our co-pilot, he said, "Hell Bob, it should come as no surprise. You had her in mind when you made the chart." So much for coincidence.

Interspersed with bombing missions was the occasional sea search. Near the southern tip of Borneo we spotted our prey. We had one sunken ship to our credit and were primed for number two. When we started our run something unexpected happened. That ship was shooting at us! Tracers flew past us and then it happened. We got hit in a fuel tank! Gas flowed out of the wing and onto the floor of the cockpit. Fumes filled the plane. Forget the immediate danger, we needed that fuel and headed for home. John, our engineer, immediately started to transfer fuel from the ruptured tank into other tanks. Fortunately we had used enough fuel that there was room in the remaining tanks to accept the transfer. During our mission debriefing at the base we were explaining the eerie circumstances when in walked a combat cameraman. I did not even know he had been with us. He presented a picture showing that our "cargo ship" was actually a Japanese heavy cruiser! Our embarrassment could not have been greater and ship identification classes were scheduled.

Late that evening the maintenance line chief entered our tent and asked if we were the crew of the plane with the busted fuel tank. We told him we were and he showed us a cylindrical metal object about four inches long. He told us he had removed it from our tank and that it was a 20 millimeter incendiary shell that had failed to explode. Don't try to tell me that God did not have a hand in the situation!

When we had completed twenty-five of our allotted forty missions, I figured that the way things were going I would make it home in one piece. I felt compelled to do something about my

Mickey situation. One of the GI's had a hobby of making small trinkets out of the aluminum skins of crashed aircraft. Some of his pieces were small heart shaped pins. I figured there was no harm in trying so I purchased one and enclosed it with a note saying that I was well and hoped that she was the same. I addressed, stamped and sealed the envelope. On the sealed flap I printed the letters S.W.A.K. In our earlier correspondence that was our way of signaling "sealed with a kiss". Corny? Maybe. But that was our habit. I mailed it and could only wait.

On the last mission that we flew to Balikpapan, I got chewed out worse than at any other time in my career. Our pilot flew with a rookie crew and he was replaced on our crew by a lieutenant colonel from headquarters. The lieutenant colonel had recently arrived from the 15th Air Force in Italy. The mission went smoothly until we completed our bomb run. The accepted practice was that as soon as the ordinance was dropped, the steepest turn possible with a formation was initiated and we got back out over the ocean. But not today! We just kept on a straight and level course and the flak kept coming. I got on the inner phone and yelled "Let's get the hell out of here."

The turn was finally initiated and the lieutenant colonel demanded, "Who said that?" Silence. "Who said that?" Again, silence. When we got back over the water, I went up and gave him the heading home and confessed "I made the comment sir." He demanded to know who I thought I was and why would I do such a thing.

I said, "Sir we had dropped our load, we could do no more harm, we were being shot at and it made no sense to me to act as a sitting duck."

He ranted and raved. He accused me of being insubordinate and lectured me on how this was a "milk run" compared to missions in Italy. He reminded me that he was in command, and on and on. At every break in his tirade I merely said, "Yes sir."

I was dismissed and returned to my navigator's table. The radio operator, who had heard the entire conversation, leaned across the aisle and said, "We all thought the same thing sir, but you were the only one to say anything."

After an eternity, I finally got a response from my "heart

pin" letter. Mickey thanked me, told me she was well and was happy that I was well and healthy. Then she said the magic words. She loved me, missed me terribly and was anxious for me to get home. This started an almost daily impassioned letter writing ritual. The letters should have been in asbestos envelopes. She loved me.

We still had missions to fly. Quite a few of them were to provide air support for invasions both in Borneo and at Zamboanga in the southern Philippines. One evening after a routine ten hour mission that day, we were playing poker about 10 p.m. when the operations officer came in and informed us that we had a 2 a.m. takeoff. The target? The capitol of Java, about seven hours flying time to the south. We made the takeoff time, the bombardier and the gunners went to sleep as soon as the landing gear was up. The pilots took turns napping. The navigator worked. We hit the target the next morning and headed for home. I calculated an estimated time of arrival, gave it to the pilot with a course to fly and I conked out. I had been up for over twenty-four hours and I was bushed.

After about six and a half hours (which seemed like ten minutes) the pilot woke me up and asked what the ETA for home was. I checked my log and when I told him he said, "That was about fifteen minutes ago and we don't see anything but water." I checked the whitecaps on the waves and they indicated the surface winds had shifted 180 degrees since we had left. A drift meter check confirmed the shift of the winds aloft. I had no way of knowing when the shift had taken place. I thought about possibilities. I really had nothing to confirm my estimates. Finally I relied on a well known military option called a "WAG," a wild ass guess. I told the pilot to turn right to a heading of 135 degrees. He said, "Are you sure?"

I was curt, "Hell no I'm not sure. Do you have a better idea?" He turned to the heading and in about thirty minutes we were home.

Our replacement crew arrived! After thirty-nine missions and 392 hours of flying in the combat zone, our tour was finished! What a great day! Almost. I had long ago dismissed my agreement to get drunk with the guys when our replacement crew arrived. I knew that the Officer's Club bar was closed since it had nothing to serve. I had heard the crew complain for weeks that they had nothing to drink, but the two ounce combat ration. I was home free, or so I thought.

Unbeknownst to me, the crew had set aside one of the twenty cases of Canadian that we brought with us. They had actually done without to save for this occasion. I was hooked. A deal was a deal.

The entire squadron was alerted. "We are going to get Wiley drunk!" About 4:30 that afternoon I settled myself in a canvas director's chair with a canteen full of ice water in one hand and a shot glass shaped like a beer mug in the other. And it started. I took a swallow of that vile, burning stuff followed immediately by a swallow of ice water. Time after time it continued. Whiskey, ice water. The guys were all game and they matched me swig for swig. Oddly enough,

I felt no effects whatsoever. Nothing. I started acting the same way as the others but it was just that, an act. My head was clear and my hand was steady. We drank to every mission. We drank to every girl we ever dated. We drank to every plan we had for those girls when we got home. About 11 p.m. I decided to find out how many of my actions were real and how many were fake. With a grossly exaggerated stagger I made my way out of the tent. I picked out a telephone pole about thirty feet away and decided I would walk straight to it. No way. Maybe my stagger was not exaggerated. The crew had accomplished their goal. I was drunk. I still thought clearly, but there was no doubt I was completely inebriated. I made my way back to the tent and flopped into bed.

Morning came and a miracle happened. I had a clear head. I had no hangover. There was no bad taste in my mouth and my stomach was normal in every respect. The other three officers were still asleep. Well, I couldn't have that. "Hey, guys, wake up. It's a beautiful day."

All three had been sick all night. They had upchucked outside the tent. They had severe hangovers and my antics were not well received. "Wiley, shut the hell up and let us sleep." I'm ashamed to admit that my revenge was sweet.

We flew a C-47 "Gooney Bird" to Townsville, Australia, to bring back eggs and fresh fruit for the troops. Then we got our orders and headed for home. We were flown to Clark Field, near Manila, to await surface transportation to the states. The only thing I remember about Clark was a little girl, about nine or ten, selling tree ripened bananas. They were small, only about the size of a wiener, but they were the most delicious fruit that I had ever eaten.

Finally, we were on a troop ship headed east on the Pacific. One day as I ate in the Ward Room, I glanced out the porthole at the beautiful blue water. A few minutes later when I looked out I saw only sky. As I continued to look, I realized that the ship was rolling. I didn't look out any more. Then I realized that the water in my glass stayed level but the glass itself rolled. I left my meal and went outside to get some air. I never became seasick but I was careful about being too observant.

As I strolled the deck, I became aware that I could see nothing but water. No land anywhere. Not even a cloud building over some unseen island. I had flown some 400 hours over these waters, but there had been a certain detachment. Then it struck me. I was thankful that my hay fever had kept me out of the Navy when I was 18!

Japan surrendered August 15, 1945. We were in the middle of the Pacific when we received the word. The air filled with the sound of celebrations on the mainland, but on shipboard there was an eerie silence. We were all happy, but most of us wondered why this could not have happened a year or eighteen months ago before we had to be put at risk.

We landed in San Francisco and the crew broke up. I bought a low mileage 1941 Ford Sedan and drove to Ogden, Utah, where Hill Air Force Base was located. My mother had been transferred there from Hanford, Washington.

I picked her up and we headed for Sioux City. We arrived on September 4, my twenty-first birthday. I was met with open arms, literally. What a joy it was to hold my sweetheart tight after almost a year and a half. I had never met her parents. Mrs. Anderson died when Mickey was fourteen. My introduction to Mr. Anderson was short. "Dad, this is Bob Wiley, the boy I told you about." Charlie was singularly uninterested. He was packing for a hunting trip and was leaving in the morning.

I mentioned three options. We could be married now and I would report for duty and then send for her. We could marry now and she could come with me. We could wait to be married when I got out of the service.

It was no contest. We decided to get married and Mickey would go with me. We agreed on September 13, my lucky number since I had returned unscathed from the 13th Air Force. Mickey's cousin would be her bridesmaid. My best friend, Swede, was away in the Navy so his brother Leonard, also a friend, would be my best man. Reverend Huff, who had known us as kids in the Glendale Baptist Church, agreed to officiate. Mary, a seamstress aunt, would make the wedding gown. My mother worked with the bride's family on the numerous details. We got the license and our blood tests. Mickey picked out and ordered the invitations. We purchased the rings, a simple gold band for me and a tiny solitaire for her.

We even had time to take in a movie. It may be hard to believe but that was the first actual single "date" that we had ever had. We had always been with a group. This was the first cash money I had ever spent on the love of my life. It would certainly not be the last.

My bride-to-be was not a diplomat. When her father returned from his hunting trip, she said nothing but merely handed him an invitation to the wedding. To say that he was furious would be an understatement. Who the hell was this punk kid who was stealing his daughter and taking away his housekeeper and cook? It was some time before Charlie accepted me as his son-in-law.

The evening arrived. The best man and I stood near the altar. The music started and a vision appeared. The bride was so beautiful that it literally took my breath away. I wasn't sure I could speak "Love, honor, and cherish... in sickness and in health until death do us part." We were now one!

Well into the reception my friends kidnapped my wife. In spite of my best efforts, I would not see her again until I was delivered to our room at the Warrior Hotel. We had to rid the sheets of cracker crumbs before we could go to bed. The wedding night of the two virgins was made in heaven!

Into the Wild Blue Yonder

Before the crew left Morotai, the squadron commander called all the navigators and bombardiers into his office and asked if any of us were interested in going into pilot training. Since I had seen the pilots alternate nap time that sounded good to me. And maybe, jut maybe; I could get a job with the airlines after I was separated. The orders in my pocket said I was to report to the base at Santa Anna, California, to be assigned to a pilot training facility.

My mother had renewed her 1920's association with Mountain Bell. She had been awarded the contract to operate the telephone office in Sugar City, Colorado.

The morning after the wedding, my mother got in the back seat of my little Ford with all our worldly belongings. My bride and I sat in front and we headed west. We dropped Mother in Denver and spent the first night of our honeymoon atop Lookout Mountain outside Golden, Colorado. The cabin that we rented had bunk beds. We only used one.

When we crossed the Continental Divide, Mickey insisted that we stop and make some snowballs. She had never seen snow in September. The trip was relatively uneventful until we approached Santa Anna. We were broke, hungry and almost out of gas. We came upon a motorist stranded along the road. I figured why not run out of gas while helping someone. When we got him to a service station he offered me a dollar for our help. I had never taken money for a favor before, but I accepted. We had enough for a gallon of gas, a quart of oil and some donuts.

I did not know where the base was in relation to the city and I did not want to run out of gas wandering around in the dark. We parked beside the road, slept in the car and stole some oranges from a nearby grove for breakfast. I reported in, got a pay check and we started married life.

We rented a room with kitchen privileges. That meant when the two little ladies who owned the place had finished eating and had cleaned up, we were allowed to have a meal. We didn't care, we were on our honeymoon.

While we awaited my assignment we visited the amusement park at Long Beach. There was a roller coaster called the Twin Cyclones. Each of twin tracks had a train of cars. The trains started at the same time. Since the course of inside track was shorter, its train got ahead of the other. The two trains were to end the ride together. In order to do that one train had to pass over the other. I knew that since I had visited as an aviation cadet. Naturally, I put us in a car that would pass under the twin coaster. When that thunder passed overhead Mickey screamed and jammed close to me. I thought it was great fun, but for the rest of our lives I never got her on another roller coaster.

I was ordered to the flight school at Goodfellow Field near San Angelo, Texas. We were fortunate to find a furnished apartment over a garage. Our landlady was very gracious. She introduced us to catfish and hush puppies. We also learned to understand some Texas talk. When she invited us into her home for "cream and cakes" we learned that was her ice cream and cookies.

Pilots used a plane called a PT-17 for primary flight training. It was an open cockpit biplane with the instructor in front seat and the student in back. This reminded me of those who flew in World War I. The west Texas winters could be frigid. We wore fur lined equipment, but nothing could keep us warm in the seventy mile an hour slipstream.

One Saturday morning about December 20 the students had just completed our weekly "pass in review." The base commander held us in formation and announced that effective immediately the school was suspended. We were to have the next two weeks off! Home for Christmas!! I called Mickey and told her to pack, we were going to Colorado. I picked her up, jumped into the Ford and we were on our way about noon. When the gas gauge showed one-quarter full, we started looking for a gas station that had a store. When we found one, Mickey went in and bought a loaf of bread, some lunch meat, fruit and some soft drinks. I was got gas, checked the oil, radiator and tires. We sped off and with few stops got to my mother's house in Sugar City about 1 a.m. We really enjoyed our first Christmas as a family.

I was one of six students with a first time instructor. The rule required that when any such instructor deemed a student ready to "solo," that student had to take a check ride with a senior instructor. My time had come.

The checker flew us out to an auxiliary field. Field was an appropriate name. It was one square mile of pasture bounded by barbed wire with a building called a stage house in the center. The instructor landed, turned the plane over to me and said, "Let's see what you've got".

I knew that when I applied power, the torque would cause the plane to turn. I anticipated that turn. Unfortunately, I applied rudder pressure the wrong way and exaggerated the turn. We were headed straight for the stage house. At the last second I saw the situation, jerked back on the stick and cleared the house by about six feet. I circled the field to land. I "rounded out" about seven feet high and when we hit the ground it was a wonder the gear did not collapse.

"Okay Wiley, try it again," the instructor told me.

My next takeoff run was straight as an arrow. I was so proud. My pride made me unaware that we were rapidly approaching the barbed wire fence. When I finally saw it, I jerked the stick back and we jumped over the fence, clearing it by about three feet. When I started to land, again I rounded out high and the landing could only be described as a controlled crash.

The instructor motioned me toward the stage house.

Well, I thought, *so ends a short flying career.* When we stopped, the instructor got out and said, "Go fly yourself. You scare the hell out of me."

After making a normal takeoff and a perfect three-point landing, I was ecstatic as I taxied in. Getting out of the plane I asked, "Sir, after those first two takeoffs and landings, how could you possibly let me solo?"

He smiled and said, "Wiley, anyone who could get in as much trouble as you did and get out of it without killing himself can fly."

∽ↄ ↄↄ

One day out of the blue, Mickey said, "Bob, I want to go home".

I was stunned. "Sweetheart, this is your home. We are married. You are my wife."

She insisted, "I know. But I mean 'home' home."

This persisted for a number of days. Finally, really irritated, for the one and only time in our married life, I shouted and cussed at my wife. "All right, Damnit, GO HOME!" Maybe something in my voice said, "And don't come back." That was the end of the conversation. Years later, as I reflect, I was wrong. I was neither empathetic nor understanding. After all, Maxine Anderson had been born in a small town in Iowa named Grant Center, which no longer exists. When she was a child, the family moved to Sioux City. She had visited her grandmothers who lived about forty miles south of Sioux City. She once attended a summer camp at Lake

Okoboji, some sixty miles northeast of Sioux City. One weekend she and a cousin flew to Omaha, ninety miles away.

With those exceptions, she had never been out of Sioux City in her life. Then I came along. I uprooted her. She had to leave her lifelong friends and her relatives. She was in a strange environment and sat alone all day in an apartment with no friends and nobody to talk to but the landlady. No wonder she longed to go home to a friendlier environment. Yes, I was wrong.

I was a very conscientious flying student. If my instructor said to go practice "S's along a highway" or "eights on a crossroad" that is what I did. Meanwhile, some of my classmates were talking about aerobatics that they had not been taught, but they had done after reading about them in their copy of a handbook we had been issued.

I figured why not give it a try? I studied the handbook and on my next free solo I climbed up to 3,000 feet to attempt a barrel roll. I got up to speed, pulled the nose of the plane up slightly and started to roll. I became so entranced with the position that I over controlled and the plane flipped over into a spin! Not to worry. My instructor had said that should this ever happen "just stop the spin with the rudder and move the stick forward to neutral."

I stopped the spin, popped the stick forward and pulled it back into my gut. Nothing. I was headed straight down. I was at 2,000 feet. I had also been taught that if this procedure failed I was to induce another spin and repeat the steps.

This I did; spin, stop spin, stick forward to neutral. Nothing. I was headed straight down. As I approached 1,000 feet I panicked. I let go of the controls and reached for my safety belt, preparing to bail out.

Suddenly the stick popped forward to neutral and the plane began to climb. Only then did I realize that in my excitement I had only pushed the stick a few inches rather than all the way to neutral. Like the old pilot in Bozeman had said, "Remember, the airplane knows how to fly". How true.

We were about half way through the primary program and I was happy with my progress. That happiness was enhanced when my new wife announced we were to become parents. Wow!! Life was good.

With the completion of primary, I was sent to Randolph Field near San Antonio for basic flight school. We flew AT-6's which had been the most advanced fighter trainer when the war started. I was introduced to instrument flying by being placed in the back seat with a hood over the cockpit. You saw nothing outside the plane and had only the instruments to show altitude, heading and speed. When I started to get used to it, it became one of the three things that I most enjoyed about flying during my entire career; instruments, formation flying, and landings. With each, I knew an immediate result. I competed with myself to become better and better.

We lived in a cabin at a tourist court with several other military couples. The San Antonio heat rivaled the San

Angelo cold for extreme weather. There was no air conditioning and my very pregnant wife really suffered. We would disrobe and I would lie next to her and her ever expanding belly on the floor and enjoy what little breeze came from a small electric fan.

I did well in basic and enjoyed it thoroughly. There was one exception; night landings. First, I made two normal landings with runway lights and the landing lights on the plane. Then there were two landings with only the runway lights. That was followed by two landings with neither runway nor landing lights. A floodlight was placed on each side of the runway. It did not illuminate the runway, but provided some light across and only slightly down the runway. When I passed those floods it was like turning on the bathroom light in the middle of the night. I was momentarily blinded. I slapped that bird onto the runway as quickly as possible, stopped, and turned on the plane's landing lights so I could see to taxi.

Basic flight training was ending and the baby's due date approached. Our good neighbors and I took Mickey on long walks. We took her on bumpy roads in the car. We did every thing we could think of to hurry the birth process. My training was over and I had about a week to report to my next station. Finally the day arrived and I took the expectant mother to Brooks General Army Hospital. After a ten hour labor we were blessed with a beautiful baby daughter.

Unfortunately I had to leave. I arranged for the neighbors to bring Mickey home and I left for Edit, Oklahoma, to attend twin engine advanced flying school. After the first weekend, each Friday night I drove back to San Antonio to be with my beloved and our new baby.

When I was about half way through advanced, I was called to a Friday morning formation. It was announced that crew training was being reduced and that half of our class would be cut. Any officer who was cut would be offered a warrant as a master sergeant. There was no way I wanted to stay as an enlisted man. I had been there. They called out names and had each man step forward as his name was called. We had no way of knowing whether the "step outs" or the "stand fasts" were the victims. I can't remember which I was, but I was retained.

Those of us who were left ferried the B-25s to Barksdale AFB, Shreveport, Louisiana. B-25's were the same type that General Doolittle and his crews flew off the U.S.S Hornet in their strike against Japan. We were able to move our families and we were back in "a room with kitchen privileges," but the three Wiley's were together and that was all that mattered.

I was scheduled to graduate in March. The preceding December Mickey and I had an auto accident on the way back from a Christmas break. We did not have time to have my 1941 Ford repaired so we traded it for a one year older model. It appeared to be a bad break, but it would prove to be a blessing in disguise.

Advanced training was relatively easy for me. Most of it was perfecting the skills we learned in primary and basic. The big difference was manipulating two engines. It wasn't a big deal in the air, but taxiing on the ground was different. The nose wheel was built like a caster and if it was even slightly off center it would cock to one side. It took me considerable practice to use throttle and brake to bring it back to center. Operating on a single engine was somewhat of a challenge. With one engine inoperative, the good engine pushes the plane into a turn toward the loss of power. The pilot uses the aircraft's controls to force a turn back into the good engine. The result, of course, is that the plane continues straight ahead, the two turns having cancelled each other out.

I got my pilot's wings in March and Mickey and I had a conference. From then on, we reasoned, we should be stationed in one place for more than a few months. We decided to buy a house trailer! Using our car as collateral, I borrowed $1,200 and bought an eight by twenty-seven foot Schulte. Here was the disguised blessing. The car that we acquired after the accident was a 1940 Ford, but it had a '46 Mercury engine and overload springs. It had been used by a Kansas bootlegger. It was ideal for pulling our new "home." I installed an electric trailer brake and we followed Horace Greeley's advice and "headed west"

to our new station, Bergstrom AFB at Austin, Texas.

I was assigned to the 7th Troop Carrier Squadron, 62nd Troop Carrier Group, Tactical Air Command. Shortly after we arrived, the group was equipped with the new C-82 "Flying Boxcar," the first plane designed specifically for dropping paratroopers and delivering their supplies by either air or ground. When the transition to the new plane was completed, the entire unit was transferred to McChord AFB, Tacoma, Washington.

Now was the test for our little red Ford. I hooked it up to the house trailer and took off for the Pacific Northwest. It performed like a champ, even over the Rocky Mountains. There was one long steep climb in Utah were we had to stop every quarter mile or so to cool off the engine and put water in the radiator, but we got there. We found a trailer park not far from the base and set up. I placed cinder blocks under our unit to stabilize it and connected the electricity.

Our home was similar to most of our neighbors. The eight foot by ten foot living room in the front had a couch and two chairs. In the corner next to the kitchen, the triangular shelves were used to store dishes. The door to these shelves was hinged at the bottom. A hinged leg hung in front. When the door was lowered, the leg supported our dining table. The eight foot by seven foot kitchen had a sink, cupboards, an ice box (not a refrigerator) and a gasoline camp stove. Later I got a kit and changed the stove over to propane.

The eight foot by ten foot bedroom had the bed, a small closet and a chest. Extra clothes were stored under the bed. All of the sanitary facilities were in a building in the center of the park. The rest rooms, showers, wash basins and the laundry were shared by all with surprisingly little conflict.

The first winter at McChord the Squadron was placed on temporary duty, TDY, at Elmendorf AFB, Anchorage, Alaska. We participated in winter exercises with personnel from Fort Lewis, an Army facility next to McChord. Another squadron from the 62nd group delivered teams of Army troops to Big Delta, a small base about forty miles southwest of Fairbanks. We picked them up there and took them to small towns like Galena and McGrath in the Alaska interior. These troops were supposed to defend the town from the "enemy," made up of Alaskan National Guard troops. Many guardsmen were Eskimo natives who hunted by sneaking up on seals and polar bears out in the open. The Army men were outmatched. After a given amount of time, we flew in and rescued the "victims" and returned them to Elmendorf to await return to Washington.

F-80s, the first jet fighters, were sent TDY to Ladd AFB at Fairbanks. They were supposed to intercept our "Boxcars" as we went from Elmendorf to Big Delta to pick up our troops. They assumed that we would fly directly from Anchorage to Fairbanks to Big Delta. If we were playing this game for real, is that what we would do? No way! So we flew low through mountain valleys where the jets could not see us. We were only sighted when we popped out on our approach to Big Delta. Fighter command was not happy.

I had been given the additional duty as public information officer. I had to make a detailed report of the operation, both the successes and problems. I did not mention the fighter fiasco. Of the entire operation, I was most proud of the fact that we never had a plane abort a mission and that we flew some 1,800 hours without an aircraft incident or accident.

We got home and resumed our training. We were still shaking out the bugs on the C-82's, normal with a new model aircraft.

The training included formation flying while jumping paratroopers of the 82nd Airborne at Fort Bragg and the 101st at Camp Campbell into a drop zone. During the summer we took paratroopers and air transport specialists to encampments of National Guards and reserve units to train, or refresh them, in airborne operations.

It was also about this time that the National Defense Act of 1947 made the United States Air Force a separate service equal with the Army and Navy. That was great, but it had one drawback. We had to buy new uniforms. Summer khakis were no problem except for the shoes. Army shoes were brown, Air Force, black. We all went to the PX, got black shoe dye and spent hours changing the color and trying to get the shoes to shine.

Not all of our flying consisted of combat training. The U.S. State Department had some sort of a lend/lease agreement with Brazil. My crew and I were directed to go to Mobile, Alabama, and pick up tractor parts to be delivered to Belem, Brazil. It was a pleasant, uneventful trip until we got to our destination.

"U.S. Air Force 7751 to Belem tower, landing instructions please." No response. I repeated the call. Still no response. Then there was a voice on the radio with a foreign accent. Holy, cow. The guy couldn't speak English and I couldn't speak Portuguese! I looked at the wind sock on the ground and guessed the direction of traffic. I got on what I assumed was the final approach, lowered the gear, dropped down and made a low pass past the tower. I flew a crosswind leg, downwind and base legs, and turned for a final approach. Bingo! The tower operator understood and gave me a green light. We landed without incident.

As soon as we got back to the States we were ordered to Fallon, Nevada, to participate in Operation "Hay lift." A winter blizzard had stranded cattle herds throughout central Nevada. The clam shell doors on the rear of our planes were removed and we were loaded with bales of hay. We flew to Ely, Nevada, picked up a rancher who knew where the herds were and directed us there. During this operation I learned two life lessons.

We picked up our rancher and he directed us to a herd of 400 or 500 head. I asked him where we should drop and he said, "Right in the middle of the herd."

I replied, "But sir, I can't fly slower than 110 m.p.h., and those bales weigh----." I got no further.

He yelled at me, "G--dammit, it's my hay and they are my cattle, and do as I tell you!"

We did as he directed. On the way back to Ely, he leaned forward and said, "Lieutenant, I'm sorry I yelled at you. But you must understand. Those cows are surrounded by snow drifts higher than their bellies. If you drop as much as five feet away from them, they can't get to the bundles and I lose the whole herd and the hay."

Lesson one: Don't question a man more qualified than

you to handle a problem.

Back at Ely, I noticed that everyone was very informal. Only a first name, a last name or a nickname was used to address one another. The exception was one elderly gentleman in a well worn sheepskin coat who sat alone in a corner. When anyone approached him it was always "Mister, So-and-so." I thought this was odd and I asked one of the ranchers to explain. "Oh, that is the guy who is bankrolling this whole operation. He just sold two of his hotels in Salt Lake City."

Lesson Two: Do not prejudge by appearances.

The Air Transport Command, ATC, did just what the name implied. They moved people and things. In peacetime or wartime they just "transport." Unfortunately, there was no love lost between Troop Carrier, a combat force, and ATC. Although not fair or justified, we said that ATC stood for allergic to combat.

Among their missions, ATC was responsible for delivery of mail and supplies within the Alaskan Air Command. In 1949, all of the C-54 type aircraft that ATC had in Alaska were pulled out and sent to the Berlin Airlift in Europe. Our squadron was given the duties that ATC did not have the equipment to perform.

On one occasion, my crew and I were sent to the ATC terminal at Ladd AFB, Fairbanks, to pick up a load of strap steel and deliver it to Point Barrow. The pieces were about an inch wide, a quarter inch thick, and about fourteen feet long. The ATC loading crew attempted to use a fork lift to move a load. With the lift at maximum height, the ends of the steel strips dragged on the ground. When the fork lift moved, the pieces fell off. Time and again. Over and over. In over four hours, only half the load was aboard. And then it happened. They quit! I asked the officer in charge what the deal was and he said, "We have a regularly scheduled ATC flight arriving and it must be unloaded."

I asked if the crew could be split and he said, "ATC loads have priority." I was fuming. "We are carrying your ATC crap within the theater. I'll give you fifteen minutes to finish my load or I'm out of here".

"Sorry, priorities."

I went in and filed my flight plan and told my crew chief to button up, we were leaving. "But sir, we only have half a load."

"We're leaving." And we did. Half way to Barrow I thought *what the hell is the matter with you? Do you know how much trouble you can be in?* It came as no surprise when I landed at Elmendorf and the line chief said that the squadron operations officer wanted to see me.

His opening words were, "Are you out of your damned mind? I just got a call from the ATC Commander at Ladd and he wants your head."

I told him the whole story, admitted that I may have been wrong, but that to be treated like that when we were doing their work really upset me.

He mulled over the situation for a few minutes and finally said, "Wiley I can understand your frustration and I may have done the same thing. But don't let it happen again."

Whew!!

Alaskan Air Command includes the Aleutian Islands. The last military facility on the mainland, before starting down the chain is a little station called Cold Bay. It sits on what could be called the "chin" if Alaska reminds you of a face. We were scheduled to "run the chain." The first stop was Cold Bay. When we called for landing instructions, the call came back, "Air Force 7751, be advised that the cross wind exceeds the maximum permitted for your type aircraft."

Rescheduling did not appeal to me. I called back, "Cold Bay tower, be advised that I have aboard 400 pounds of mail and packages for Cold Bay personnel." There was a very long pause.

"Roger, Air Force 7751. Land at the pilot's discretion."

I fought that bird onto the runway, understanding the cross wind warning. I was pleased with myself, but not for long. As I taxied in, I passed a B-17 with three big red stars under the cockpit window. It was the plane of the commander of the Alaskan Air Command. And to make matters worse, standing there, sheltered by his plane, was the man himself. As I walked past him, on the way to base operations, I saluted him and he said, "Isn't it a little bit windy, lieutenant?"

"Yes sir, it is" and I kept walking. Again, whew!

Back at McChord, the Squadron Commander called me in and dropped a bombshell. "Wiley, you are a hell of a pilot and we are sorry to lose you, but you have been transferred to the Wing Headquarters Legal Office."

Disappointment and Opportunity

The legal office? Were they nuts? They were telling me to leave what was arguably the best crew in the 62nd Group? Here were three dedicated, efficient guys: crew chief, radio operator and a cargo handler who was an apprentice mechanic.

One evening when we were on maneuvers with some National Guardsmen we had an engine quit. I landed safely. The squadron commander called McChord where group kept a built up engine on a pallet for quick deployment. He was assured the engine would be shipped overnight.

The crew chief asked me, "Sir does this mean we can't go into town tonight?"

I said that if the bad engine was removed and the plane was ready to have the replacement installed, they could go. By 10 a.m. the next morning, we flew a test hop with the new engine. Then wing directed me to give up these troops for a desk job in a legal office. I was gravely disappointed.

In the new assignment I was a claims officer. We processed all claims against the government; household goods damaged in shipment, automobile accidents involving government vehicles, and aircraft noise that effected farm animal production of eggs and milk. I diagramed vehicle accident sites using the skills in mechanical drawing learned at Woodrow Wilson Junior High School. And that was not the only connection with the Sioux City school system.

Once a claim investigation was completed, it was sent to the wing commander for review, approval and signature. Evidently the former claims officer had trouble with sentence construction. The old man was incensed. He put out an order, "Find me someone who can write a decent report." Mr. Erickson of Central High influenced me to select English/Speech for my college major and that showed up on my records. The commander had his man. Unfortunately it was me.

I continued as claims officer, but I also became somewhat familiar with the Uniform Code of Military Justice. There are three types of courts martial. The Summary Court is for minor offenses and is conducted by a unit commander. The Special Court is for the somewhat more serious offenses and is conducted in front of a panel of officers by a trial judge advocate or prosecutor and defense counsel. The General Court Martial, for more serious crimes, has the same court setup as the Special Court but with the addition of a law officer, who must be an attorney. I started working in Special Courts, first as a defense counsel and later as a TJA. It was a great learning experience.

My boss, a member of the bar, was hard to get to know. He was competent, but almost withdrawn. I was surprised one day when he called me into his office and said, "Bob, I have to leave for a week or two to act as law officer, judge, in a general court martial. You are familiar with everything here and you will be in charge. If something unusual comes up, think it through, make a decision and DO something. I don't want to come back and have a pile of unfinished work on my desk."

As it turned out something unusual did come up. There was a conflict between the provost marshal and the legal office. This was not unusual since one represented law enforcement and the other the law. As the boss had directed, I studied the situation, made a decision, and took action, much to the displeasure of the PM. When the boss returned, I briefed him on everything that had happened during his absence, including the conflict.

A few days later, I was sitting outside the wing commander's office waiting to get some claims forms signed. My boss was receiving the worst chewing out that I had ever heard and it concerned the actions I had taken during his absence. I sneaked out without being seen and returned to the office to fearfully await the judge's return. When he got back, he went directly into his office and did not say a word.

A week or so later, I spoke to him on another matter. He interrupted and said, "Oh, by the way, that matter between you and the sheriff; what you did was perfectly reasonable, but if the same situation should arise in the future, you might also consider so and so." There was never a word of reprimand or fault finding. From then on, I held him in much higher esteem.

Our daughter was about three and I mentioned that we had elected to have two or three children. Mickey agreed but insisted that she would not have another baby while living in the trailer. We sold it for the $1,200 we paid for it in the first place. We made the down payment on a two bedroom $8,000 house and furnished it completely with the rest of the money. We shopped estate sales, flea markets and Goodwill stores. We got unfinished furniture and I finished it to please my bride.

True to her word, Mickey became pregnant. Whether this was to fulfill her wish or to get out of tending the garden I will never know. When she went to the hospital at Fort Lewis, we agreed that I was to take some leave to babysit our daughter and paint and wallpaper the whole house.

I finished both bedrooms, the bath and was just finishing up the living room when she called and wanted to come home. I said I thought she was supposed to stay one more day and she started to cry and say I didn't love her or want to be with her. Nothing could be farther from the truth so I went out and picked up her and our second daughter. When we got home she was very pleased with the way everything looked. Then she opened the swinging door between the living room and the kitchen. It had not been touched. There were cobwebs over the dirty dishes in the sink. She laughed herself silly and for the rest of our married life she never let me forget.

About this time I was promoted to captain. That was great, but it caused one of the few disagreements that my wife and I ever had. The raise in pay was only $45 and I said, "Honey, we have been living on a first lieutenant's pay, why don't we just invest this raise?" The roof just barely stayed intact! I had never seen her so mad.

"Bob, don't you understand? We need this, we need that, we can't even afford so and so. Do you want us to live on the edge of poverty?"

I promised her that when I got promoted to major, that entire raise would be hers. The argument was to no avail. I did not realize that the next raise would not be for five years. Did you ever feel like you had lost when you had won? I did. I insisted we start saving NOW. You could have chopped the air with an ice pick at the Wiley's the next few days, but she finally accepted the situation.

At work I was presented with a daunting challenge. I was selected to be the TJA on a general court martial! Four years before an enlisted man had stolen and sold twenty-five type-writers from the base typing school. He was arrested and an Article 32 investigation resulted in an indictment. He was being held in the stockade pending court martial when he escaped. The FBI finally located and arrested him and returned him to military control. The charge of desertion was added to the existing charges. Before he could be tried he escaped again. This time he was recaptured in Olympia,

Washington, about sixty miles from McChord. The case was handed over to me to prosecute.

We had to retrieve all the paperwork that had been completed four years before. All the witnesses had to be located and subpoenaed. My boss was very helpful in directing me to the appropriate law books and case citations. I was ready to go even though I felt a little nervous but there was some self-confidence there too.

In spite of its magnitude, the case was relatively easy to prosecute. The family of the accused had hired a defense attorney who was a former judge advocate in the Navy and was thoroughly conversant with the military justice system. The staff who had handled the case four years ago had done a great job of assembling documents and evidence. The two charges of Escape from Confinement were proven by military records, as were the periods of absent without leave, a prerequisite for proving desertion. The absences had to be accompanied with the intent not to return. That intent was obvious because the accused was apprehended over 2,000 miles from his assigned post, with a changed name and had been married under the assumed identity. The serial numbers on the stolen typewriters were identical to those found in the buyer's warehouse. The buyer testified that the accused represented himself as a USAF Salvage employee, selling units that had been replaced by newer models. The verdict was guilty on all allegations. I felt that justice prevailed when the accused was sentenced to a dishonorable discharge, forfeiture of all pay and allowances due or to become due and fifteen years imprisonment at Fort Leavenworth.

Not long after the trial, I was called to the wing personnel office. The officer asked me if I was a Colorado native. I told him I was. He said, "They need a squadron commander for the Headquarters Squadron of the 4600th Air Base Group at Ent Air Force Base in Colorado Springs. The man slotted for that assignment has asked to be relieved. Are you interested?"

Is there a stronger word than absolutely? It was a dream come true. "Yes Sir!" was my reply.

Then he stated the "not so good" conditions. It was Thursday and I had to report to the Springs on Monday. I was excited, but when I told my wife she was shocked. But she said, "Dear, if that is what you think best."

I left Friday morning with the only family car, leaving Mickey with no transportation, a four-year-old, a six-month-old baby, and the responsibility of selling the house and arranging to have all our household goods shipped. She did not utter one word of complaint!

The 4600th provided support for the Headquarters of the Air Defense Command. I thought that Ent was some acronym, but the base was named for General Uzal. G. Ent, a wartime commander of the base.

Whenever I had spare time, I would look for a suitable dwelling for my family. I was not meant to be a bachelor. When they arrived, we moved into what had been a groom's quarters over a stable behind an old mansion on the north side of Colorado Springs. We were very comfortable there until we had time to shop for a regular home to buy.

When I reported in, I was pleased to find that I had a career master sergeant as my first sergeant. Some may call him "Sarg," but I called him my right arm. After all, when a kid from Kelly Park was placed in command of over 300 airmen, he needed all the help he could get. This "Top Shirt" had a favorite saying. "Sir, one hand washes the other."

Since I had been a GI I had empathy for my men. By the same token, I expected top effort from all. I tried to be fair, but I may have been harder on some of the laggards than I should have been.

With the kids in tow, Mickey and I spent evenings and weekends looking for a suitable home. National Homes was building new homes in an area called Stratton Meadows. These houses had all the interior and exterior walls, and the roof manufactured out of state. The parts were assembled and placed on a concrete slab. There were three bedrooms, one bath, living room, a kitchen with an eating area and a utility room. We really liked the house and it could be assembled in less than three weeks. We bought the house that would be our home for almost five years.

I had commanded the squadron for about nine months when the base commander called me into his office. "Wiley," he said, "ADC has directed that your squadron be commanded by a field grade officer, a major."

I said, "Thank you sir, I am glad for the promotion." He smiled, shook his head and replied, "Sorry. No such luck. I am reassigning the major that is my director of operations and training to the squadron and replacing him with you."

I was both disappointed and delighted. A staff position! It carried prestige, but it was no walk in the park. Shortly after the transfer, I prepared a letter for the commander's signature and presented it to the base adjutant for review and delivery. He was "old Army," pre World War II.

"What the hell is this trash," he bellowed. "Don't you know anything about being a staff officer?"

"No sir," I replied, "But I'm willing to learn." The old guy melted like an ice cream cone on a hot day, took me under his wing, guided me and helped me during our entire relationship.

Owning a new home was great, but it took a lot of work. I built a redwood fence and planted the lawn. I connected a garden hose to the drain on our washing machine and ran it into a sprinkler. We had the lushest lawn in the neighborhood. I built a garage with direction from a friendly neighbor. In it I had a shop and it was wired so I would have lights so I could work at night. I had studied and felt confident when I installed three way switches to control current from either the house or garage. I called the neighbor over to observe my electrical triumph. I threw the switch in the house. Nothing. I tried the switch in the garage. Nothing. I was crushed. I studied the directions. I checked each connection. Everything seemed in order. Then my "friend" turned on the switch in the garage and reached up and screwed in a light bulb. Perfect! The dirty dog had unscrewed every light bulb in the garage just to give me a hard time yet, we remained close friends until he died twenty years later.

When I assumed my duties as director of operations and training, I studied all the applicable Air Force regulations. I then wrote implementing instruction for those that applied to our unit. I established reporting requirements including a submitting schedule. My secretary did all the filing of reports. I had a lot of idle time.

Now that we were settled, we could fulfill one of my wife's wishes. We got her a Wurlitzer Spinet piano and arranged for her to take voice lessons. We had sung together in the choir at the old Glendale Baptist church, but she had been unable to get into the choir in high school. Girls from some of the more affluent families had a distinct advantage since their parents could afford voice lessons. I was proud and happy that I could do something for my bride that was just for her.

I got tired of just sitting around. I went to the base commander and said, "Sir, I don't have anything to do."

He said not to worry; he would find plenty for me to do. And did he ever. My first project was to upgrade the Base Children's Nursery. When I entered the small existing facility, the urine stench was overwhelming. Children with wet diapers sat on the wooden floors and toddlers who were not yet totally potty trained relieved themselves at will. This was not going to be easy.

There was an empty "H" shaped barracks that I got permission to use. Two normal sized barracks had been built parallel to each other about 20 feet apart. The bar of the

"H" that connected them contained a wide hall and rest-rooms. At the end of one of the buildings was a room that was normally used as quarters for the senior NCO. The nursery was considered a "non- appropriated fund" activity and no government money could be used in its operation. Maintenance of the building, including paint and floor covering, was authorized. Since we had no funds, the base commander and I signed a note and got $600 from the bank.

Through a friend I contacted four interior design students at the University of Colorado. I invited them down and we had lunch at the Officers' Club. I told them my goal of having an attractive, safe place where military families could leave their kids while the parents shopped or attended a social function. We would furnish the labor and materials, but the students could select paint and floor tile colors. Their budget was not to exceed $300.

Several proposals were submitted. We opted to paint the walls and ceiling in the play area in pastel colors. The NCO quarters that was our office was finished in green. The floor tile was white, interspersed with red tiles that formed a trail a toddler could follow. The students suggested that several cutout paintings be installed. I remember one of them depicted a clown guarding a box which was to hold toys.

Nap area walls were painted a restful blue. The ceiling was the color of a dark night sky. Later on the staff installed silver stars and a big orange moon. Window shutters matched the ceiling. The kitchen and restrooms were painted in white, semi- gloss enamel.

I had a gated fence installed at the entrance, just outside the office. I did not want children on their first visit to fear being fenced in when the gate closed. I had two bears as tall as the fence made out of plywood. One was painted brown, the other white. One was mounted on the fence and one on the gate. When the gate closed, they came together and appeared to be shaking hands. This established the "The Teddy Bear Inn." I was relieved and gratified by the overwhelming favorable response from the mothers of our wards.

The NCO wives held a fund raiser to help us buy toys and playground equipment. I consulted an expert in equipment of this kind. Given our client's age was it better to buy swings, a slide or monkey bars? She suggested that we build several saw horses, each about eight to ten inches high and two feet wide. Then she told us to get some two foot by eight foot pine boards about six feet long. We sealed these to prevent slivers.

The kids loved it because they could climb Mount Everest in their minds using the saw horse. A plank atop two saw horses made a perfect trail for follow the leader. The combinations were endless!

Maybe it was Shakespeare who wrote something like, "Hell hath no fury like a woman scorned." Obviously the writer had never crossed the wife of a General. She barged into my office and introduced herself as the General's wife. She informed me the Officers Wives Club planned to have a nursery benefit fund raiser. She ended with, "And of course, we will have free nursery that night."

I said I appreciated the support, but that free nursery services were out of the question. She exploded, "And why the Hell not?" I explained that the NCO wives were not given a pass and it would not be fair to grant a free night to the officers. "Captain, don't you realize that you are one of us? Have you no loyalty?" I was unmoved. "Young man, have you ever heard the phrase 'Enmeshed in his own chicanery, heist by his own petard.' If not, look it up. And she stormed out. I did, in fact, look it up. A petard is the sash that a pirate wears around his waist. If he becomes a traitor to his crew, they use his petard to hang him from the yardarm.

Later that evening, a friend of mine was sitting at the bar in the "O" Club. So was the General. In stormed his wife ranting and raving about that "damned ungrateful nursery officer. He would not even allow a free night when the benefit was for his Teddy Bear Inn. "And do you know why? Just because the enlisted people did not get one.

My friend told me that the General finished his drink and said, "Good for him." I felt fully vindicated.

In December 1953 the mother of my two daughters presented them with a baby brother. We named him Dennis after a comic strip character called Dennis the Menace. His middle name was Charles after his maternal grandfather. With the middle initial "C" he fit right in: Diana Lee, Deborah Dee and Dennis C.

Since I was no longer on call for the nursery, my evenings were open. I took the opportunity to join The Ent Players, actors from the Air Base Group and Air Defense Command

Headquarters. After performing in one play, I was cast in a second. We had just started rehearsals when a problem arose. One of the players was a lady named Babbette. She was the wife of a good friend of the family and, I will admit, her looks did justice to her name. One night after rehearsal, the cast stopped for ice cream and I brought Mickey a cone. As she was eating it she said, "I don't think it's fair. You go out and have fun and stop for ice cream and I have to sit home with the kids." There was no accusation, but I could sense the "green-eyed dragon" lurking behind the statement. My true love certainly had no cause for concern, but to put her mind at ease I dropped out of the play.

The Air Installations Office was responsible for the design, construction and maintenance of all roads, sidewalks, utilities and buildings, as well as fire protection. The officer in charge had been sent to Korea and the base commander assigned me as his temporary replacement. I had just become marginally familiar with my duties and the folks in my office when a little man from the ADC Headquarters Inspector's office came into my office and said, "I have just shut down your work on the Peterson Field hangers. It is a serious fire hazard." I did not have a clue what he was talking about, but I said I would check it out and give him a call.

"Pete" Field was the flying and warehouse area located several miles east of Colorado Springs. Several of the hangers pre-dated World War II. I discovered that one of the inspectors from my office had found deterioration in some of the joists supporting the roof in several of the hangers.

My engineers had devised a plan to bolt six foot lengths of channel iron, deep enough to cradle it, to the joist. All of the channel iron pieces were welded together so they could reach the exterior bearing wall.

After some review, I was uncomfortable to see that the contractor who had been awarded the job had submitted a bid of over $15,000 less than his closest competitor. I found out the reason was that he was welding the channel iron pieces together after they had been bolted to the wooden joists. All the other contractors were assembling the pieces on the ground and hoisting them into place with a crane.

I could see the risk of welding next to wood so I met with the contractor and the fire chief. They explained the procedure they were using, it made sense to me, and I invited the little man from ADC to join us. The fire chief explained, "Before the channel iron is in place, we use a two inch hose and soak the joist. During the welding, I have a fireman with a live hose standing next to the welder. As soon as the weld is finished, we flush the area. We keep a manned fire truck in the building around the clock. In my opinion, it is perfectly safe."

The pipsqueak sputtered, "Well, not in my opinion." He turned to me and said, "If anything goes wrong, I will see that your career ends."

I "invited" him to leave and to stay away from my project. He stormed out. I turned to the contractor and my fire chief. "You heard him guys, my butt is on the line. Don't let me down." The project was completed successfully.

The new air installations officer arrived and I returned to my "Mickey Mouse" projects. These included a command-wide skeet shooting competition, a golf tournament at the Broadmoor Hotel and I served as Air Force liaison officer to the Pikes Peak or Bust rodeo. That lasted until ADC established a protocol office and I was placed in charge. I had a secretary and a female enlisted person. We had two primary functions. Our office controlled the only unlocked entrance to the building. Every vendor, visitor or employee who had forgotten a key, had to be identified, registered and given an ID badge. Our other job was to coordinate all major conferences. We made sure that VIP's had suitable quarters. Transportation had to be coordinated. We put together the information packets for all participants.

A major conference was scheduled with attendees from the three number Air Forces under Air Defense Command. Everything was in order. I spent the day before the meeting at Peterson Field so I could meet each arrival. I gave each the packet of information and asked that, because of the number of attendees, all should go directly to the 0900 hours meeting at the theater and not visit the Headquarters building. It was the middle of the night when the last arrived, so I slept at base operations.

The next morning, I went to the theater. When the meeting was underway, I sighed with relief. Everything had gone smooth as silk. I called Dorothy, my secretary, to tell her I was going home to shave and shower. She broke into tears and said the base commander wanted to see me. What?

Before I went to see the boss, I wanted to know why. When I got to headquarters, I learned why. It was a horror story.

The female enlistee was supposed to open the office at 0730, but she had gone AWOL to see her boy friend at F.E. Warren AFB in Cheyenne. Every vendor east of the Rockies had to deliver that day. A number of the conference attendees had chosen to ignore my request and they went to the headquarters building.

When Dorothy got to work at 0800 the line outside the building was over a half block long. She worked feverishly, with help from a fellow officer from next door. Too late. General Benjamin Wiley Chidlaw (yes, Wiley), commander of Air Defense Command drove past the building, accompanied by the commanding Generals of the Three Numbered Air Forces under his command. Here was a long line of people trying to get into his headquarters. Undoubtedly, he was embarrassed. When he got inside, he saw the chaos in my office and demanded, "Who's in charge here?"

"Captain Wiley, sir."

Then he asked, "Where is he?"

"He's not here sir."

General Chidlaw turned to his chief of staff. "Fire him." Fired! On the spot! By a three star General!

After the Firing

Dorothy was still sobbing as I prepared to leave for the base commander's office. I gave her a hug and told her not to worry. Who was around to tell me not to worry?

I walked in, saluted and said, "You wanted to see me sir?" He motioned for me to sit down.

"Wiley, I think you were doing one hell of a job. I hope that you understand that I have no choice but to relieve you."

"Yes sir. I understand." Then the thunderbolt!

"What would you like to do?" he asked. A miracle! Could this be true?

"Well sir, I would like to get back to a flying job and I think jets are the future of the Air Force."

He punched his intercom and called in my friend, Charlie, the base personnel officer. The boss said, "Chuck, get Bob a slot at the T-33 jet transition school at Yuma."

Charlie turned to me and said, "Do you have any single engine time since you got out of school?"

"Nope."

He turned back to the colonel and said, "Sir regulations require that a man have some fighter time before he can transition into jets."

Without changing expression or voice level the boss said, "Maybe you didn't understand. I said get Wiley a slot at Yuma." Then he turned to me and said that when I got back I would be assigned to base operations at Peterson. We saluted and left.

When we got out in the hall, Charlie turned to me and said, "Wiley, you bastard, do you know what a bind you have put me in?"

"Hey buddy, don't blame me. He just asked me what I wanted to do." We were still friends after Charlie did what appeared to be forbidden.

I was pleased with this new opportunity. I was excited to be training in a jet. I was definitely not impressed with Yuma in the summertime when temperatures routinely topped 110 degrees. Even though there was an 11,000 foot runway, we did not fly after 1100 hours because the heat decreased the density of the air to the extent that we could not become airborne.

The T-33 jet trainer was basically an F-80, our first jet fighter. The cockpit had been lengthened so two pilots sat in tandem. For initial training the student sat in the front seat. With instrument flying training, the instructor sat in front with the student in the rear under a hood that limited the view to inside the cockpit. Trainees were supposed to get "cockpit time" which meant just sitting in the cockpit with the plane on the ground, to study the position of all the controls and instruments. When I say supposed to get, that meant almost never. Sitting in a cockpit with the temperature at 114 was unreasonable. I would catch up on this back in cool, colorful Colorado.

With jet training completed, I went to work learning the varied responsibilities of a base operations officer. It was great to be back among fellow pilots. I got a lot of delayed cockpit time and flew the T-33 locally at every opportunity.

About this time, Colorado Springs was selected as the site for the new United States Air Force Academy. I was selected to lead a flight of three "T-Birds" on a low level flight past a landmark called "Cathedral Rock" on the academy site. The flight was featured on a Grantland Rice sports movie short. Don't be misled by the fact that I led the formation. My fighter pilot buddies insisted that I lead since they did not trust me to fly as a wingman.

The assignment was great, but it came with a problem. With the headquarters job, many neighbors were also assigned there. If Mickey needed our one car any day, a friend who went to work at the same time would give me a lift. But not many guys had jobs at Pete Field. On numerous occasions my wife would have to drive me to work dressed only in her nightgown and house coat. A neighbor was imposed upon to watch the kids. This system was not acceptable. I bought an ancient Buick for a couple hundred bucks. It ran and that's about all, but it served its purpose.

The base had B-25's and T-33's, both of which I was qualified to fly. I had to take transition training in the C-47 "Gooney Bird" because I was unfamiliar with the plane. I became an instrument flight instructor and check pilot, and ultimately the head of the instrument school.

Life was good until a shock came. A letter was issued stating, "The following officers, not having been in combat are alerted for shipment to Korea." I was stunned. No way could this go unchallenged. I studied the situation and found, what I thought to be, the flaw in the system. Pilots' flight records are kept in a folder labeled "Form 5." Other flight crew members were recorded in "Form 5A."

Naturally, since I had not become a pilot until 1947, no combat was listed in my pilot file. My 392 hours in a combat zone were reflected in my "5A." I showed both files to the base commander and said, "Sir, I am a career Air Force officer and if it is my turn to return to combat I will go. But if the reason I am slated to go is because I have never been, that's wrong." He agreed. He took the case to ADC. They acknowledged the oversight and removed my name from the alert, as well as eleven other officers in the same situation.

Most of our B-25s had been modified to carry five or six passengers. Those of us in base operations flew non-rated VIPs to inspections and official visit stateside. These doctors, attorneys and accountants appreciated not having to fly commercial. We flew at their convenience.

I was flattered that the General who was the command surgeon always asked for me to fly him. I always did my best to meet his schedule, including one instance that nobody in authority ever found out about. We were scheduled to take off for return to Peterson Field. My co-pilot and I went out to taxi the plane in position to load. The starter on one engine was burned out! Disaster! A replacement would not be available for at least two days. Unacceptable! What could I do? I did something that I have never admitted before.

I borrowed a tug, the little tractor used to move planes on the ground. I scrounged a long piece of nylon rope. I wrapped one end of the rope around the hub of the prop. I tied the other end to the tug and backed up to take the slack out. I set all the switches and cockpit controls in the "start" position. My co-pilot got in the cockpit and I told him, "Buddy, this is a one shot deal. If it fires don't let it die." I backed up the tug as fast as I could, the prop spun, the engine fired and started! We took off on time and no word of this highly unorthodox procedure was ever mentioned. Thank goodness.

Truthfully, I liked to fly with the General. At every base we were afforded first class treatment. Ground crews and motor pool personnel gave us the best possible service. And I think the General appreciated the professionalism of my co-pilot and me. Until one day.

We were to take the General to a national medical convention in Boston. When I checked the east coast weather conditions before we took off, things looked suspicious. A fast moving cold front was headed for the Atlantic. When we got to Ohio, I contacted flight service for the latest

Boston weather conditions. High winds with peak gusts in excess of thirty-five miles per hour. Over West Virginia, reports showed the weather deteriorating rapidly. When we reached western Massachusetts, the Boston weather was rain, limited visibility, high winds and numerous vicious tornados.

I turned to the General and said, "I'm sorry sir, but it's not safe to proceed and we will have to go to our alternate airport."

"Captain," he said, (Captain, not Wiley) "It is imperative that I get to that convention."

"Sir, in my estimation it is even more imperative that I keep you safe and alive and keep this plane in one piece." When we landed at the alternate, he was obviously furious, but he said nothing. After we returned to Peterson, I never again flew with him.

A few months later, I learned that the General was in a T-33 flown by a young lieutenant that landed in a snow storm at Kirtland AFB, Albuquerque. They ran off the end of the runway. The hand print of my former passenger was all over that accident. It was too bad that the kid forgot that he was the pilot and he was empowered to make all decisions regarding the operation and safety of his plane.

It has been said, "All good things must come to an end." That was true for me when orders were published sending me to Iceland for a one-year tour. Amid the condolences from my friends, initially I felt very sorry for myself. Then I got real. After all, I had just spent almost five years at one base, almost unheard of in the Air Force. And it was in the beautiful state of my birth. I had had opportunities to work with great people, superiors and subordinates, on various interesting assignments. But, Iceland?

I was surprised to learn that the average mean temperature there was within a few degrees of Colorado Springs temperatures. Even though it is far north, it is warmed by the Atlantic Ocean's Gulf Stream. According to history (or legend) the Danes, on their discovery maps, reversed the names of Greenland and Iceland. Greenland is truly a land of ice where a glacier virtually covers the land.

My wife was a great cook. When we got married, I had just returned form overseas and I weighed 175 pounds. Within six months I was up to 192. I stayed there for about ten years and then I hit 215. I am six feet tall. When she kissed me good bye for my trip north she said, "Honey, while you are up there, why don't you try to get down to the weight you were when we got married?" I had already agreed to learn to drink coffee, so I agreed. She would learn to regret that request.

The trip was relatively uneventful. I was routed through New York City and I had a chance to ride the subway. It was a simple thing but an experience for a kid from Kelly Park. A bus took me to McGuire AFB, New Jersey. I boarded a plane and headed north. I cannot say that I was disappointed when I first glimpsed Iceland because I had no particular expectations. I was shocked by the stark bleakness, black earth dotted with huge black boulders. It was June, but I saw nothing green. No grass, no shrubs, no trees. Later on, I learned that nothing grew at Keflavik except some tiny flowers. I noticed these little things only because their bright petals stood out from their black surroundings.

After I checked in and moved into my quarters, I reported to Iceland Air Defense Headquarters and was assigned to the Plans Division. I soon learned that we did no planning. We just monitored reports of the status and levels of pre-positioned fuel and supplies. These were for forces that would be deployed in the event of hostilities with the Soviet Union.

That was it for our office. No decisions. No challenges. No planning. Nothing. I thought that a reasonably bright twelve-year-old could have done my job. What made matters worse was the attitude of some of my fellow officers. Some of them kept muttering, "I hate this (bleeping) place."

That got on my nerves to the point that one day I lost it. I bellowed, "None of us are happy here but bitching doesn't help. When you are around me, just shut the hell up!"

Then there was the standard answer when I asked a question concerning my job. "Wiley, up here we just play it by ear." Don't get me wrong. I was not a stickler for following the letter of a regulation. I had been known to put a liberal interpretation on the obvious intent to make a decision based on a poorly phrased sentence. But these guys did not have a clue as to what a regulation directed. It was always, "Wiley, up here we play that by ear." Finally, I made a sign that I put on my desk and pointed to it when that phrase was used. "Before you try to play by ear, make sure you know the tune."

For the first time in my military career, I felt that I was stuck in a job that was boring drudgery.

The tasks that Mickey had assigned progressed swimmingly. I had learned to drink black coffee. The weight loss program had a regular routine. Six days a week I skipped lunch. I ran from the office to my room and changed into my gym clothes. I ran to the gym and joined fellow officers in volleyball for an hour. Then I ran back to the dorm, showered and changed clothes, and walked back to the office. My lunch "hour" stretched to almost two.

There were bright spots. One was when we were treated to a concert by the nationally famous St. Olaf College choir. They laid over a few days enroute to a European tour. I was proud to be selected to fly an octet to an outlying aircraft control and warning site.

Some ten years later after I had retired, I was helping a young couple with three children find a home to rent. During one conversation, the young father mentioned that he had attended St. Olaf. I told him of my octet flight and he said, "Oh, yes, I remember that trip well. I was in the choir, but I did not make the side trip. My cousin did and she told me how much she enjoyed it." This family man was a college student when I was stationed in Iceland? Suddenly, I felt very old.

The command conducted a flying safety contest in early November. The winner was to get a fifteen day leave which encompassed Christmas. Virtually everyone entered. The winner would be announced in December. The wait was an eternity.

Humor is a great balm during conditions when there are nineteen or twenty hours with no sun. Just after Thanksgiving, a Jewish friend of mine bought some packages of construction paper. He cut one large letter from each sheet. He fastened the letters to a heavy string about fifteen feet long. He hung his handiwork in the dorm hall. It read "DECK THE HALLS WITH MATZO BALLS."

All troubles were forgotten in early December. I won the Flying Safety Contest!! When I got the time frame for the leave, I called my buddies at Peterson Field Operations and asked them if they had any trips scheduled about the time I would hit the states. They agreed to meet me at Steward AFB, Newburg, New York, near West Point. My flight landed at Logan International Airport, Boston. I took a train to New York and another north to Newburg.

By the time we got to Colorado Springs I had been on the road for about forty-four hours. I was unshaven, my skin pallor reflected the lack of sunshine and I weighed the requested 175 pounds. As I got off the plane, my dear wife's words were, "Bob, you look awful!!" It was the most memorable Christmas of my life.

This trip back to "The Rock" was different from the initial deployment. This time I knew what waited. There were no families for IADF personnel. This contributed to the most common forms of diversion: getting drunk and bedding some of the Icelandic women. But there was a third alternative. Education. The University of Maryland kept professors in Iceland to teach regular classes. I managed to accrue six hours of transferable college credits in Economics. We started with Adam Smith and continued through the Depression. The hardest part of school was getting there and back. One night after class it rained as hard as I had ever seen. The wind was blowing so hard that one could hardly stand. Every once in a while I had to step behind a building or telephone pole, protected from the wind, to rest. I wore a hooded parka that reached my knees. I had boots that reached mid-calf. In the exposed area between the two, the wind blew the rain through my pants and down my legs. When I got to my room, my socks and shoes were soaked.

One winter night we were sitting in the Officers' Club relaxing after dinner when the base operations officer came in and asked if any C-47 pilot was sober enough to fly. It seemed that a six-year-old Icelandic boy was in a life threatening situation. He had to get to the hospital in Reykjavik, the capitol, some thirty-five miles away. The one road was slick with rain water and was not safe for high speed driving. I had always made a point to never volunteer. This was different so I raised my hand.

The plane with the little passenger aboard had its engines running. The maintenance line chief had taxied the plane to the front of operations and was sitting in the co-pilot's seat. We took off without a flight plan and headed east. There was a slight mist and the cloud ceiling was about one hundred feet above the ground. We flew at about fifty feet. After a few minutes we saw the lights of the capitol and the rotating beacon of the airport. When we landed, an ambulance was waiting. The next day we learned that the boy had survived and that his condition was stable. That was indeed gratifying.

It was a beautiful spring day so a friend and I checked out a plane for an aerial tour of the island. I was surprised to learn that Iceland's agricultural area was around Akureyri, a town in the north central part of the island, not far from the Arctic Circle. Then I figured out why. There was rich, volcanic soil, the climate was warmed by Gulf Stream breezes, and in the growing season there were twenty hours of sunshine with virtually cloudless skies. One was reminded of the Matanuska Tundra in Alaska.

My tour was coming to an end when Air Force Headquarters initiated Operation Carousel. It directed that any flying officer, who had not flown as a regular crew member for five years or more, would be sent to Strategic Air Command for crew duty. Off "The Rock" and back with a crew. Life was good!

"SACumcised"

When my orders came, they assigned me to the SAC base at Columbus, Ohio. I was to fly B-47's which, at the time, was the most advanced bomber in the Air Force inventory.

When I got back to Colorado Springs, I contacted my mother. While still managing the contract telephone office, she had gotten a Colorado Real Estate Broker license. We listed our home with her to sell, arranged for our things to be shipped, piled the kids in the car and headed for Ohio.

Until our Colorado home sold we had to live in a rental. We found a small, nice, three bedroom place not far from Lockbourne Air Force Base. "Nice" except for the cockroaches! By the HUNDREDS! When I turned on the light at night, the floor was literally covered. We had to be careful where we stepped. We sprayed, painted baseboards and used a fly swatter. We were very grateful when our old home sold and we were able to move into a new tri-level. As a precaution before we occupied our new home, we applied all the same anti-roach products.

When I reported in, I was assigned to a strategic reconnaissance squadron. I was sent to McConnell AFB, Wichita, Kansas, for B-47 training. It was daunting. The largest plane I had ever flown was the B-25 and here was this monster that, when fully loaded, could weight over 220,000 pounds. And it was a new design. It was, to my knowledge, the first swept wing aircraft and those wings flexed up over fourteen feet before the plane became airborne. The landing gear consisted of two sets of wheels located under the fuselage, one in front and one in the rear. It was referred to as "bicycle gear." Years later, I learned that the plane was the most difficult to fly in the entire Air Force. I don't know if that was true, but it was a handful and I was grateful for patient instructors who got me qualified.

Shortly after returning to Lockbourne, I was promoted to major. As promised years before, that monthly increase in pay went to Mickey. She put it to good use buying a three piece sectional couch and a pink marble coffee table, both of which I still have in my apartment.

Before I became fully familiar with strategic recon, the unit's mission was changed to electronic counter measures, ECM. The squadron was re-equipped with Phase V B-47's. All of the bombing equipment was removed from the bomb bay and a pod was installed containing an array of ECM equipment. Our wartime mission was to join a bomber stream and protect the strike force by "jamming" and making enemy radar ineffective; ground tracking, anti-aircraft tracking and enemy fighter tracking. The crew was expanded from three to five, adding two ECM Operators.

I could not have hand picked a better crew. Mel, my co-pilot, was a rebel from Ole' Miss. He was my good right hand. He logged and managed our fuel. He used a sextant for celestial shots for the navigator who could not see from his position in the nose. Mel was our gunner, handling the fifty caliber tail guns.

Nick, my navigator, had been on a select crew before leaving the service briefly to accept a lucrative civilian job. It bored him and he came back.

Ed, the ECM officer, had been an instructor in a navigation school. He plotted celestial fixes along with Nick. Each would do his own work and they would compare. My guys could run a celestial mission that was comparable to one using radar. "Moon," the EMC master sergeant, had been a radio operator flying "The Hump" in the CBI theater during World War II. On more than one occasion, Moon isolated radio problems on our plane when ground crews could not. They were a dream crew in my estimation.

I will interject here the SAC crew structure. There are four steps; Not combat ready, combat ready, lead, and select; N,R,L,S. Each designation is based on level of competence and experience. Competence was judged by a standardization board or "stand" board. Virtually no deviation from the "standard" was tolerated. That may have been the basis of the seemingly derogatory term "SACumcised." You did have to give something of yourself to the SAC mission. No "hot dogs" or "cowboys" allowed. The mission was to maintain the peace and the SAC motto was "Peace is our profession." With thousands of aircraft and hundreds of missiles located worldwide it was a finely tuned operation requiring precision execution. Even on training flights, our takeoff roll had to start within twenty seconds of the scheduled time or the aircraft commander had to explain the deviance in writing.

My challenge was aerial refueling. We normally cruised at Mach .74, 425 knots, at 25,000 to 28,000 feet. The speed of the KC-97 tanker, loaded, was 200 Knots at 11,000 feet. Directed by my navigator, who had radar contact with the tanker, I would descend to a point 100 feet below and 100 feet behind the tanker. At these slow speeds, the controls were very sloppy and slow to respond. When our refueling checklist was complete, Mel would notify the tanker. The boom on the tanker was lowered by its operator and he would direct us to come in. There were fins on the boom and the operator could fly it up and down and left to right. New pilots, such as I, have a tendency to "chase" the boom. We soon learn to virtually disregard the boom and merely fly formation with the tanker. As we got in closer the boom operator would direct "Up three, forward five. Down one, forward one" as appropriate. He would then extend the boom and place it in our refueling receptacle where it would latch and the fuel would start to flow. I had to keep the receptacle within a four foot "box," two feet up, two feet down, two feet left, and two feet right. Outside that area, the boom would automatically unlatch and retract. This would happen so quickly that the boom operator could not stop the fuel flow until my canopy was awash with fuel. Then the whole process had to be repeated. There is a great feeling of satisfaction the first time you take on the full 30,000 pound fuel download without a single automatic disconnect.

In a relatively short time we were deemed combat ready and ineffective designated R44V. That designation came with a price. We were now due for our stint in the "mole hole." This was an underground bunker where crews stood alert for a week at a time. No contact with the outside and subject to the sound of a claxon, twenty-four hours a day, sending us scrambling to our "cocked" aircraft to await the either the word "launch" or "practice." We did a lot of route and target study, but we also played a lot of pool and ping pong.

Each colander quarter every crew position had to accomplish certain minimums; so many fifty caliber rounds fired, so much refueling, ECM practice runs, and celestial and precision navigation (radar) missions. On board cameras and ground radar sites recorded everything and it was all reviewed, logged and evaluated by the stand board.

The only black mark against my crew came at my expense. We were scheduled for a night "mass gas." Nine B-47s were to fly in loose formation. We were kept in a straight line and about a half mile apart by our navigators using radar. In a designated refueling area, nine KC-97 tankers, in a similar formation, awaited our arrival. Everything went well until the tanker force commander called and cancelled the mission due to bad weather.

Our leader directed us to proceed on our alternate missions. Just as we were about to do so, our designated tanker called and said he had just broken into the clear and asked if we would like to complete the refueling. My navigator had the tanker in radar contact so we said, "Okay." and started our descent. I have failed to mention that we had a stand board observer aboard who had climbed aboard just before takeoff. What a great break for us! We save a scheduled mission when all other crews had "finked out." I latched onto that boom and we were in business. The tanker commander called and said we were about to leave the refueling area and he was going to make a 180 degree turn. I hung on that pipe without a disconnect and we took on our scheduled fuel load. I thought the evaluator had to be impressed. Nick called on the interphone, gave me a heading and our estimated time to "Springfield." Mel was filling out fuel logs so I called the traffic control center and relayed Nick's information.

The center acknowledged and asked, "Which Springfield?" I knew we were in Missouri so I answered, "Missouri." Nick immediately called me and reminded me that the ECM radars we were supposed to jam were in Springfield, Illinois, just across the Missouri River. I called center with the correction and we got our clearance.

The next week, I saw the stand board report. They cited my error as "poor crew coordination." I appealed to the colonel in charge and asked that he cite my mistake as mine alone and asked that it not reflect on my crew. But it was to no avail.

My crew was selected to participate in Operation Reflex. This was a program that sent crews from various units to England to stand alert and augment crews assigned overseas. As soon as we arrived at a base north of London, we cocked our plane and were on alert for a week. We were then given a week off. That was followed by another week on alert before returning home. After the first week, the crew decided to go to the continent. I thought it would be good for them to get away from me for a week. I told them I had to go into London on an errand for Mickey, which was true.

My bride had heard of the London silver galleries. She had given me a piece of our silver service flatware and asked that I find a silver service and tray to match. I found the galleries and more specifically Langford's of London. They had been in business since the mid 1600's. I told a young lady my request and in a short time she found a matching tray and tea service from some time in the 1700's. The tea service had the tea pot, sugar bowl and creamer, but no coffee pot. It seemed that when this service was made, coffee was not popular in England. She looked for almost an hour until she found a coffee pot for a "marriage." One had to look very closely to find the minute differences in the pieces. When she asked about payment, I told her I had only enough money to last me until I returned home. I had made notes and told her I would send for the order or pick it up on my next visit.

When I returned to my hotel that evening there were two wooden crates addressed to me from Langford's. This young lady had known only my name and my rank since I had been in uniform. She guessed my hotel since it was one most often used by the U.S. military. She did not know my unit or home station. She did not know the type aircraft I flew or my temporary duty station in England. You talk about blind trust!! For months after I got home Mickey and I would send $50.00 every month or so and an occasional $100 until the bill was paid in full. How could you possibly betray such a trust?

The flight home was memorable. For the first time, we were to refuel at altitude from a KC-135 jet tanker. What a difference! We hooked up at normal cruising speed where the controls are very sensitive not the sloppiness you have at lower speed and altitude. To say the least, I over controlled and it was a rough ride. When we broke off I apologized to the crew, but Moon came on the interphone and said, "No need to apologize, sir. The last time I had a ride like that I had to pay a quarter for it at the county fair."

When we got to the states, the weather at Lockbourne was bad and we had to land at a SAC base on the East coast. Unfortunately, that set the stage for the first, and only, dissent among the crew. The aircraft commanders of the other five returning B-47s ordered a minimum fuel load for a direct flight home. You have the same, time consuming preflight inspections for a long or a short flight. I asked the crew what they each needed to complete their quarterly requirements. Every requirement could be completed in little more than an hour extra flying time than a direct flight. I told the crew we would finish our quarterly requirements. The tension was palpable. All crew members except Mel were married. We had been gone for most of a month and they wanted to get home. So did I. But we would not have to fly any more during the rest of the quarter. We will never know whether that tension filled flight was a factor, but shortly thereafter SAC waived the "six months as a ready crew" requirement and we were designated a lead crew, L44V. Forty years after I left the crew we had a reunion in Omaha at the SAC museum. Every crew member remembered the incident clearly.

A call into the squadron commanders was something to avoid. When I reported, he said, "Wiley, they need an experienced aircraft commander to train as a controller in the Eighth Air Force Command post. You are to report Monday for a week of evaluation."

Great, you work to have a top crew and they jerk you off for a desk job. I've been there, done that.

When I reported to Eighth, the officer in charge said, "Well Wiley, what do you think of an opportunity to be at the headquarters?"

He, like I, was just a major. "I think it stinks," I replied. "I would rather stay with my crew." He smiled and told me we would talk after a week of indoctrination. I worked with various crews on each of the three shifts. I both observed and, under supervision, performed a number of tasks. Friday afternoon I met with the chief controller. He asked what I thought now. My attitude had not changed. "I think it stinks. I would rather stay with my crew." When I got to work at Lockbourne on Monday morning, I was handed orders to report to 8th Air Force Headquarters, Westover AFB, Springfield, Massachusetts. So much for choice.

Once again I had to leave Mickey and the kids. We listed the house and, again, it was a depressed real estate market. A defense plant in Columbus had closed and the city was flooded with for sale signs. I stayed on the base at Westover and, on weekends, looked for a home for my family. After about a month I found a great place and, being fed up with living alone, called Mick and told her to pack up and come. For about six months we had to make two house payments. Sure it was hard, with financial consequences, but I had my family with me. It was worth it.

The work at the underground command post was interesting and challenging. We monitored the alert status of all SAC bases in the eastern United States as well as Goose Bay, Labrador. We controlled all SAC aircraft being deployed over the Atlantic and monitored all other USAF aircraft being deployed. We had three shifts; 7 to 3, 3 to 11, and 11 to 7. We worked each shift for two days and had two days off. The controller on the 11 to 7 shift had to brief the General staff on closed circuit television at seven each morning. I could not see them, but they could both see and hear me. You covered all pertinent activity during the previous twelve hours and answered any questions they had. It was daunting initially, until a coworker reminded me that they could seated on a commode. With that picture in mind, briefing became easier.

The home I picked out was in South Hadley, a suburb of Holyoke near Springfield. It was a Dutch colonial with a barn like roof that came down to the wall of the second story. The house, like old Carlin Street, sat on a plateau half way up a moderately steep slope. There was a street on the top of the hill with a driveway leading down to the garage. The front driveway led from the garage down to the street in front. There were doors in both the front and back of the garage. When I came home from work on a stormy night, I would park the car on the upper street and walk down the snow covered driveway and open both garage doors. When I drove down, I would do my best to keep from skidding and slammed on the brakes when I got in the dry garage. It may sound goofy, but it worked.

The shift work suited me. I had a lot of time off while the stores and lumber yards were open. We redecorated and did some minor remodeling.

Evidently I was not kept busy enough. Mickey became pregnant! With our youngest almost seven, Mickey was not happy AT ALL! She refused to buy maternity cloths, making do with some of my clothes. The kids were convinced that they would starve to death with Mom in the hospital.

When that warm, soft, baby head touched Mickey's cheek, I think she finally forgave me. I had not finished a project when she insisted on coming home. I made a bed for her and the baby in the dining room. My wife actually laughed when she saw the toilet from the upstairs bathroom sitting on the top of the stairs.

My tour in the command post was relatively uneventful with one grave exception. We had nine KC-97 tankers from Homestead AFB, Florida, on their way to Goose Bay, Labrador, to relieve tankers who were on alert there. The weather man came to me and said that by the tankers arrival time, frontal weather would close the base to landings. If that were to happen, they would not have enough fuel to get back to an alternate airport. I briefed the "on call" General staff officer and told him I thought best to have the planes land at the nearest SAC base, refuel and continue. He concurred. All nine deploying tankers were ordered to land, refuel and continue to Goose Bay.

Then, big trouble! Three planes developed mechanical problems and could not continue. Two others ran out of crew rest. SAC regs prohibited crews from taking off if they had been on duty for twelve hours or more. As luck would have it, the weather cleared at Goose Bay and the final four tankers arrived with no problems.

I briefed my lieutenant colonel boss in detail as to what had happened and I covered the basic facts in the closed circuit General staff briefing. About this time, the commander at Goose called 8th Headquarters raising particular hell that he did not have a full complement of replacement tankers. He said the weather had never gotten bad and he wanted somebody's head.

The director of operations at headquarters called my boss and the spineless SOB said, "Sir, Major Wiley was on duty. He can explain," and he put me on the phone.

I explained the situation and my thought processes in detail. When I got finished, he said, "Wiley, don't you agree that you made a mistake?"

"No, sir, I do not. Given the weather information I had, and thinking of the safety of the planes and crews, I would do exactly the same thing again."

There was an eternal pause and then he said, "Well, okay." and hung up.

My pipsqueak boss slapped me on the back and said, "Congratulations. As tough as he is, an okay is like a commendation medal."

I thought *thanks a lot, wimp. Why could you not speak up on my behalf?*

After just under two years at Westover, evidently someone in SAC Headquarters in Omaha saw on my record that I had been in "Plans" in Iceland. I was ordered to the directorate of plans and programs at the "head shed." Here, at last, was an opportunity to do some actual planning.

The decision had been made that SAC no longer needed forward bases in North Africa and Spain. We had to formulate plans for the redeployment of the alert aircraft as well as the orderly withdrawal of personnel, supplies and equipment. Then there had to be a plan to return control of the bases to the host country. There were "Status of Forces" agreements between governments and care had to be taken that those treaties were not violated. Daunting? Yes. Challenging? Yes. But it was a real satisfaction when each step was accomplished.

Ever since the late 50's and early 60's I had a sense that my mother's health, both mentally and physically, had begun to diminish. Since we were her only family, when I got to SAC Headquarters I applied for a "compassionate transfer." There was a missile unit just east of Denver and since I had had command post experience, I hoped for a favorable decision.

Unfortunately, one of the considerations in granting such a transfer is the prognosis of the patient. Recovery had to be reasonably expected within two years. Her doctor wrote that, at her age, such a prognosis was not possible. Request denied.

I felt I had no choice but to seek an early retirement, well short of the thirty years service I had planned. Fortunately, I had been promoted to lieutenant colonel in only five years instead of the seven it took to go from captain to major.

In civilian life, there is little demand for an operations staff officer so I had to make some plans. The obvious answer was to go into real estate. My mother's business was dormant but she still had an office. That was a start.

I enrolled in the University of Omaha and started taking night classes. The Air Force had a program called "Operation Bootstrap" where they paid for your college courses. The catch was you then had to remain on active duty for a period of years. Since that was not acceptable, I had to pay my own way which did not do much for the family budget. I studied Real Estate Principles and Practices, Real Estate Management and Business Law. My mother told me that

Colorado had just passed a law that was going to require that a person spend at least two years as a salesperson before he become a Broker. The last Broker exam before the law went into effect was October 1963. I had to take the shot and I took a few days leave to go take the exam. Fortunately, in my college courses I had learned enough to pass and I just put my new Broker license on the inactive list until I was able to retire.

One of my friends asked me if I was going to get a degree. "Are you kidding?" I joked. "I'm almost forty-years-old. Why would I need a degree?" He talked me into talking to my counselor. The counselor said he would do some checking for me. He evaluated my grades from Iowa State Teachers College, from Montana State when I went through air crew training and the University of Maryland while in Iceland. Then he allowed credits in meteorology and math from my navigation and pilot training. He then recommended several end of course examinations which I took and passed to get additional credits.

He then said, "Well Bob, you have credits for a major in Military Science and a minor in Business. But you have to have a second minor." I asked for a suggestion. "Well, you have Economics credits that you earned from the University of Maryland. You could pick up six more hours there."

I knew nothing of labor relations or collective bargaining, but I earned three credit hours in each and I was granted a BGE, Bachelor of General Education degree. They sent me my diploma after I had retired.

I was slated to retire at the end of July. On Memorial Day, we drove to Aurora, Colorado, a Denver suburb, and looked at models of homes being built in several areas that mother had scouted. We settled on a bi-level four bedroom in a new area called Village East. We picked colors for brick, trim and carpet. I told the contractor I was to retire in sixty days and asked him if he could complete the home on time. He assured me he could.

I retired on July 31, 1964, having completed twenty-one years, two months and seventeen days service to my country.

Winding Down

We closed on our house in Omaha and made arrangements to have our household goods moved. By the time we got to Aurora, it was August 3. I called the contractor and asked if the house was finished. He assured me that it was, but that varnish on the hardwood floors could use another day to set. We stayed with my mother that night.

After living as nomads the first twenty-nine years of our married life, we were moving into what would be our home for the next twenty-nine. From the front door, seven steps led up to living room, dining room, kitchen, full bath and two bedrooms, one of which I would use as an office. From the entry, six steps led down to two bedrooms, a recreation room with fireplace with raised hearth, a three quarter bath and utility room. To me, it was more than ample and all we could afford. It was the lowest priced home in the area and it took a while to overcome Mickey's desire to have one of the larger homes which cost $15 to 20,000 more.

My business office was in the converted, one car attached

garage at my mother's home. There was an entrance from the front porch so a client need never go through her home. She could get to the office directly from her kitchen. It was an ideal setup. We each had a desk and a phone. She would be the receptionist and bookkeeper. That activity and responsibility had an immediate, notable effect on her mental health and attitude. Much of the first few weeks I spent studying literature on sales and marketing and familiarizing myself with the Denver real estate situation. I learned, years later, that 1964 was the worst market since World War II. Oddly enough, to me it was a blessing in disguise.

The Martin Company had closed its plant and fired or transferred its employees. The real estate scene was flooded with GI and FHA foreclosures. These were all listed in the Denver Post on a weekly basis. Any broker could sell any one of these properties, would be paid a commission, and his buyer had built in government financing upon qualification. It was a wonderful opportunity and learning experience.

Since I was gone so much in my years in the military, I had my paycheck sent directly to the bank. Mickey had the checkbook and managed the bills. Any life insurance or investment payments were done by allotment before the net proceeds were deposited. My retirement pay was calculated using my base pay and my years of service. They took away my flight pay and my housing allowance and I got 52.5% of the base pay. My first retired paycheck was about half of what I had been making. Mickey panicked. "We just can't make it. What will we do?" I tried my best to assure her that everything would be okay, but to no avail. Finally, I took over the check book. Then she relaxed and thought everything was fine. We had no more money than when she controlled the purse strings, but "out of sight, out of mind."

My retirement pay covered our mortgage and our food. That was it. But we survived until some real estate commissions began to come in.

For the first few years our living came from the GI and FHA sales with an occasional individual listing and sale. Then the Washington bureaucrats stepped in. All brokers were called to attend a meeting at the Denver Federal Center. They announced that, effective immediately, all contracts for the sale of government foreclosed homes would disclose the race of the buyer. I asked why. They said it was to discourage discrimination. I argued that to avoid discrimination it was important to only consider a person's name and financial status in qualifying. The rule would stand. I announced that I would never again sell one of their properties. And I didn't. Did I cut off my nose to spite my face? Possibly, but I felt it was a matter of principle.

Shortly thereafter, I got my first big break. My attorney said that he had a hog farm on the north edge of the Denver metro area and some of the larger real estate firms had been unable to sell it. Would I like to try? Absolutely!! I gathered the information on the property ran an ad in the paper and had a large for sale sign painted and installed. Almost immediately, one of the larger firms contacted me. We submitted a contract to my attorney which offered full price, cash, but with a contingency that they be given a short period of time to assemble a real estate syndicate or joint venture. A number of investors would pool their funds, purchase the property and hire a manager. The manager would oversee the property, collect and pay expenses, but the investors, by a majority vote, would determine any development or disposal of the property. We closed on the pig farm and, more importantly, I learned how to establish and manage a joint venture.

Residential real estate sales is an adventure in people.

Early on I learned that I could not sell, but I had to find out what folks wanted and help them find it. And the last thing one should do is interject a personal opinion. A minister called me to help him sell a house that he had rented for years. He had completely renovated the property and, in my opinion, it was beautiful. He had installed high quality royal blue carpet in the living room and dining room. For a small home, everything was spectacular. I had been looking for a home in this area for a young family with two little boys. I picked up the wife and I was excited for her. When she walked in the front door she stopped and gasped. "Did you ever see such hideous blue carpet in your life?" My lesson: |Keep you opinions to yourself.

Mickey could not have been happier. With me home to watch after the kids, she could pursue her musical aspirations. She auditioned for, and was selected, for the chorus in the Denver Post presentation of *The Sound of Music*. The Post series was held in outdoor venues during the summer.

The contact with other chorus members led her to the company at the Bonfils Theater. She had an occasional solo but sang in the chorus of, among other musicals, *Sugar*, *The Red Shoes*, *The Apple Tree* and *Kismet*. I was pleased to see her having so much fun.

The real estate business is what I call "chicken and feathers." You can do well for a time and that is followed by frequent "dry spells." I had to augment our income.

In certain areas of Aurora there is a soil condition called bentonite. When exposed to water this type of clay swells, and causes structural damage to any structures sitting on it. Some homes, subject to such damage, are abandoned and existing loans foreclosed. I found such a home and located a contractor who gave me an estimate to renovate the building and correct the drainage so that future damage could be avoided. The cost would be $4,000. I borrowed $11,000 from the bank to buy the property and took the plunge. With the job completed, I put the home on the market for $19,500 and within three weeks we closed for $17,500. It was only a $2,500 profit but it helped the family income stream. Three years later I listed and sold the same home for $20,500 and made a commission on that sale. Life was good.

In 1968 Charlie, Mick's Dad, retired. He had made pretty good money as a machinist, but he thought more about cars, guns and boats than he did retirement. He moved to Aurora to be near his daughter. He rented a mobile home and I could see the handwriting on the wall. Sooner or later he was going to need some help. We surely could not support him, but something had to be done.

While reading business publications I learned of portable miniature golf courses. They were built on two foot by four foot frames, topped with four foot by eight foot plywood sheets, carpeted, with two by two pieces of wood along the sides. They came with a caddy shack and the usual obstacles, e.g. windmill, light house, church, etc., nine holes in all. Mickey and I flew to the Pennsylvania factory to see the finished product. I asked Charlie if he would like to work for me and he agreed. I negotiated a ground lease on a highly traveled street on the back side of a shopping center. I borrowed the necessary funds from the bank using as collateral the investment we had made years before when I was promoted from first lieutenant to captain. I took out a $25,000 life insurance policy with the bank as beneficiary so Mickey would not have a burden if something unfortunate happened. I hired two other retired men and paid all three the maximum they could earn without jeopardizing their Social Security. The course was open from April through October, but I paid them the year around. In the fall they would move the obstacles into the basement of the shopping center and in late February and March they would repair and paint the obstacles before returning them to the course in April. When Charlie got married and moved to Arizona, I sold the course. The annual payments covered the room, board and tuition for our youngest son to go to college.

I had put together several small, successful real estate joint ventures. A very affluent friend was aware of this. He approached me and said he and a group of investor friends were interest in purchasing a five acre tract of land on South Federal Boulevard in Sheridan, a small suburban city south of Denver. They did not want their names known for fear that if the owner learned who they were; he would jack up the price. Would I be interested in putting together a joint venture to complete the deal? What an opportunity! I approached the owner and presented myself as "acting for an undisclosed principal," a well recognized real estate practice. The owner agreed to sell for one dollar a square foot, but would not pay a real estate sales commission. I returned to the group with that information. I told them that in lieu of a commission I would accept a ten percent interest in the joint venture, a value of $10,000. They agreed, a bank loan was obtained and the deal was closed. My share of the payment on the bank loan was $147.00 a month but I was to get paid $50.00 a month to handle the book work.

What I did not know was that the group had already lined up a thirty year non-subordinated ground lease on the back two and a half acres of the ground for the construction of mini-warehouses. Long after our loan was paid off, that monthly lease rent came in handy. The lease included an option for the tenant to buy the ground in the twenty-fifth or thirtieth years of the lease. With ground values continuing to rise, I could see that I would get ripped with taxes if that were to take place. Mickey and I kept two of my ten percent interest and we gave the other eight percent to our kids or grandchildren. Diana, unmarried got two percent. Kevin, Debi's only son got two percent. The two children of both Dennis and Dan each got one percent. Not much each month but when the option to purchase was exercised, it was somewhat substantial.

Mickey still sang, but she had started to develop asthma. This led to her first major health problem. She had been treated with iodine drops and the dosage had increased to fifteen drops a day. The treatment caused a "thyroid storm." She was hospitalized and placed on a 6,000 calorie a day diet, but she continued to lose two pounds a day. She was finally stabilized and started using inhalers which proved a satisfactory treatment.

A friend at church owned a low income rental property in an industrial area. He wanted out and hoped to buy a motel in Colorado Springs. I bought the property for $1,500 and I assumed three mortgages. There were six old cabin camp units, ten mobile homes on blocks, a three bedroom house, and a wash house with machines for which I was paid a portion of the rentals. Over time I renovated the entire complex which my kids called "Dad's slum landlord property." I replaced all the windows in the cabins since most of them would not even close. I replaced the dangerous space heaters, installed an entire new electrical distribution system and paved the area which had been all dirt. I was fortunate to have an honest, competent manager. To assure that I kept him, I made a move that friends said I was crazy to do. I bought a ten foot by forty foot mobile home and placed it on a vacant space. The manager and his family moved into it and loved it. I told him that if he just paid space rent and stayed five years, I would give it to him. He was elated. He had never owned a home. Truth be told, his space rent made my payments on the mobile home and it was a "win, win" situation.

In the early 1980's my mother began to make an occasional mistake with the books. I assured her that they could be corrected easily and that she should not worry. Finally, she said, "Bob, I think it is time for me to retire." I said that if that was her choice, I would just move my office into my home. It had been a most congenial partnership.

In July 1982, I had just gotten back to my office after lunch when Mother called. "Bob, come take me to the doctor."

"What's the matter?"

"Just come!"

When I got to her home she had severe chest pains and was as mad as I had ever seen her. She was furious that "that little bit of digging in the garden would bring on something like this." I got her to the hospital and after she was stabilized she started giving orders.

"Take my rings. I don't want people to be tempted. Pick up Duke (her dog) at the groomer. The slip for my cleaning is on the kitchen table." When she was stable, I left and did as she had directed.

That night, after watching the news, I called the hospital

to check on her condition. The chaplain said it may be better for me to come to the hospital. I consulted with the doctor and told him of her wishes. She died at 2 a.m. July 8, 1982.

She always insisted that funerals were "pagan" and that she wished to be cremated and her ashes spread in the mountains. Her wishes were granted. I firmly believe that the last few years of her life were the happiest and most care free of her life. She lived alone with her dog in her own home. She still drove. At 80 she was still square dancing. She was still independent and she avoided her greatest fear; living in a nursing home. As I gaze at the Rockies I remember the scripture "I look to the hills from which cometh my strength."

My wife wanted to go to work. That was especially true when things were tough during our early retirement. Right or wrong, being of the old school I always thought that the husband and father should be the breadwinner. When our youngest was in high school I started to reevaluate. Was it really fair to take a chance that Mick would become a widow and a worker at the same time? I relented and she went to work in a Veldkamp Flower Shop. She was a natural. She loved and knew flowers. She was very sharp and picked up the business details quickly. She planned to work just twenty hours a week. Because of her ability with customers and her personality, twenty soon became twenty-four, then thirty-six, then forty.

One morning when she was getting dressed for work she said, "This is the pits. Do you know what it is like to get up and go to work EVERY day?"

I assured her that I had "been there, done that" and she just giggled. After a month or so, going in and out of the cooler made her asthma worse and she had to quit. Then she got a job delivering singing telegrams! After thirty years of marriage and four kids, when she showed up in an office in a Playboy bunny suit, her figure still turned heads.

When we arrived in Aurora, it was a nice city of some 40,000 people. The borders were controlled and the growth was gradual. All in all, it was a nice situation. I became interested in the city government and became a member of the Citizens Advisory Budget Council. It soon became evident that the current mayor was incompetent and he pushed for vast expansion of the city I believed harmful. Some folks even accused him of being crooked but I saw no concrete evidence of that. For almost two years I encouraged friends and contacts within the government to run for the mayor's office. My efforts were fruitless. Finally I decided to run myself.

I knew nothing about running for office. I read books, talked to friends in government and garnered all the information I could. I formed an organization and filed the required paperwork.

There were four candidates; the incumbent Mayor, two members of the City Council and me. One of the most gratifying events for me was when I appeared before the Aurora Board of Realtors. When asked, I told them of my plans for controlling rampant growth of the city. A friend walked out of the meeting with me and said, "Wiley, what the hell is the matter with you? You are one of us and you want to control growth?"

I replied, "You guys asked me a question and I gave you an honest answer. Did you want me to lie?" About a week later, that same friend called and invited me for a cup of coffee. As we sat down, he pushed a check for $200 across the table. When I asked him what the deal was he said, "After you left, we got to talking. We all agreed that you told us what you thought. All the other candidates said what they figured we thought. We admired that. Good luck." That made me feel good. I lost the election, but I beat the mayor and one member of the City Council.

After the election, an acquaintance came up and asked me for some advice on running a campaign. I laughed and told him to ask someone else that I had lost. He said, "But I liked the way you ran your campaign." We chatted and I shared ideas. He became a state representative, the state treasurer, the Colorado secretary of state and is serving his second term as a U.S. congressman.

While serving on the budget committee I met a man who owned Industrial Realty Company. We became friends and he supported my mayoral run. I learned something of his business and one day asked him if he had a management division. He said that he did not but that he had been thinking of adding one. In short, I joined IRC and took over management of about two million square feet of warehouses. It was an interesting challenge.

The owner of a majority of the property we managed

was a multi-millionaire who lived in Dallas. For years he had been a friend and mentor of my friend, the owner of IRC. The money man, in my opinion, had been taking advantage of IRC. If our company negotiated a lease on one of his properties, he paid a leasing commission but then expected us to manage his buildings for nothing. I was having none of that and, somehow, convinced my boss to stand up to his old mentor. We started collecting a small percentage of each lease payment.

One of the Dallas owner's small buildings was about twenty—five-years-old and the parking lot was in terrible shape. I asked for permission to have it repaired but he said, "That is the tenant's responsibility. Read the damned lease."

I agreed, but argued that if he had not enforced the lease provisions for twenty-five years and had not required preventative maintenance, it was not fair to stick the current tenants with complete replacement. He said he would consider it and I obtained, and submitted, a bid for about $20,000. I heard nothing.

For almost a year I did my best to maintain the parking lot. I would load hot asphalt from the plant in my little pickup and fill the worst chuck holes. One day I called Dallas and said I was going to submit a bill for a new pickup. Mine had fallen into a hole and broken an axle. Of course that was a pure fabrication, but it got his attention. He asked if it was really that bad. When I assured him it was only a slight exaggeration, he sent his son and his son-in-law up for a first-hand look. When they confirmed my evaluation, he agreed to resurface the parking lot.

This was about 1978 when we hit the first oil crisis. The new estimate was over $40,000, twice the original. I should have felt sorry for him, but I didn't.

A constant problem in a warehouse area is the presence of pigeons. They nest under the eaves of buildings and their droppings stain the sides of the buildings. You cannot legally destroy them, but I did manage to reduce their numbers. A pest control company had corn laced with a hallucinogenic. The birds become disoriented and could not find their way home. One day my boss said, "Bob, you have to clean up such and such a building." Look in the yellow pages and see if you can find a pigeon droppings removal company. What to do. Finally, I decided to rent a self-propelled lift. I went to the Denver Fire Department and borrowed about 300 feet of two inch hose and the wrench for a fire hydrant. Not a very dignified way to make a living, but it was effective. And the tenants were very appreciative.

I had been with IRC for almost six years. I enjoyed the work and got along well with the tenants. My friend, who owned the company, was generous and giving. Christmas parties were lavish and bonuses were more than adequate. But, always a but, he was very hard to work for. He was very controlling. If I saw that something could be done quickly and easily I would do it only to be told, "That is not your responsibility." He and some friends owned a new building. As building manager, I alerted the tenants that the parking lot was to be resealed at their expense. They appreciated the "heads up" so they could plan the expenditure. When the boss returned from a trip, he exploded. "I will decide what should be done to my building." Like I said, he was, and still is to this day, a good friend. I did not want to jeopardize that friendship by having a business clash.

I was approaching retirement age so I went to the Social Security office to check on my potential benefits. They figured my payments at ages 62 and 65. I thanked the lady and started to walk out. She asked if I was going to apply. I said I would wait until I was 65 to get the higher payment. She told me to sit down and she did some calculations. Finally she said, "Mr. Wiley, if you delay for three years it will take you twenty-seven years at the higher rate to make up the loss. I signed up and told the boss that I would retire the following September. It was March and I wanted him to find and train a replacement. I reminded him of my pending retirement in April, in May, in June and July. He took no action. In August I was emphatic. My birthday was September 4.

He said, "You mean you really are going to retire?" I did my best to indoctrinate my replacement and introduce him the tenants. I left IRC on my birthday.

Although it was controlled, Mickey's asthma was getting gradually worse. She also began having symptoms of rheumatoid arthritis. She did stay active and sang in the church choir as well as the Aurora Singers. After a fundraiser for the group, she was selected to send thank you letters to the major donors. She sat at the typewriter in my office, laboring to write each note individually. I showed her how to use the computer so that all she had to change was the name, address and amount. I wrote down the steps to take and monitored her first successful effort. I returned a few minutes later and she was back at the typewriter. To be kind, she was not highly technically skilled.

When I told the family of my pending retirement, our youngest son asked what I planned to do. I said I didn't know for sure but that I would probably work in my shop, work in the garden and maybe do some amateur acting.

"You acted?"

"Yes, until your mother asked me to quit when she was alone at home with the kids." He said they really needed older men in the Denver area to make television commercials and industrial films. He talked me into auditioning for an agent. She signed me up and I started going to auditions. I refused to join a union so work that I did was paid for, but I received nothing for residuals. I had fun, learned a lot and met a lot of great people. Being in front of a camera was no big deal since I had done so when briefing the General staff from the command post at Westover. I did this for a number of years. I made a few bucks, but I just considered it a hobby that paid for itself and a little bit more. Our son talked Mickey into doing a few, but she was so much of a perfectionist that she did not enjoy it.

Our oldest son was working in a liquor store and one day he approached me and said, "Dad, the guy that owns this store is a drunk. He spends most of his time in a bar a few doors away. He doesn't pay the distributors and they only sell him second grade product and for cash on delivery. There is a great upside potential and a good chance to make money. You might be able to buy the store at a bargain."

I told him that I had had no experience in the retail business and I didn't even drink. He said he knew the liquor business and that I had been a businessman ever since I had retired. I agreed to think it over.

As a real estate man, one of the first things you learn is location, location, location. I had to agree that this store was ideally located. It was at the intersection of two main arterials and accessible to each. It had a drive-through and it had businesses that shared the parking lot. Inside the store was not clean and the most shocking thing was that there was a six inch stack of unpaid invoices on the counter. I started our due diligence. We checked everything; rent, insurance, maintenance, utilities, everything. Except sales. The man had no records! Finally, I went to the city and checked the sales tax records. I found that each January the store had been shut down because the taxes had not been paid, but then the fees were always paid and the store reopened. Using these figures as a guide, my son estimated that gross could be increased by at least $20,000.00 a year. We had a plan. We would run the store for five years. In that time we should accumulate enough capital that we could buy the building. Mickey and I would take title to the building and our son could have the business. He would pay us a reasonable rent and everyone would win. We borrowed $35,000 and bought the Sub-S Corporation that was "Powderhorn Liquors."

The first order of business was to upgrade the product in the store. I contacted every distributor. Some were willing to start delivering quality product on a COD basis. Some I agreed to pay ten cents on the dollar of unpaid invoices. They were happy to do this since many had already written off a loss. All this was being done without Mickey knowing the details. If she had known of the $35,000 loan, she would have flipped.

The brother of a friend was developing a computer program and equipment to read the bar codes on products. He needed a site to do beta test, the final step before putting it on the market. We were glad to oblige. As a result, we were the first liquor store in Aurora to be able to scan prices rather than enter each by hand. I spent hours and days putting bar codes into the computer. We also acquired a computer that kept books, tracked inventory, and recorded purchases, markups and margins. We cleaned up the store and made it attractive. Our daughter's father-in-law came to visit, stood near the counter with his hands behind his bat and mused, "Yes, this is a gentlemen's store."

At the end of our first year of operation, it became apparent that the former owner had lied in his sales tax reports to the city. Our gross was about $20,000 short. As a result, it took us a full year of growth to get to what we anticipated would be our starting point. As my son predicted the continued growth was there, but we fell short of our goal. At the end of our planned five years, I asked him how much he wanted for his half of the business. I doubled that figure, added the current value of the inventory and the cost of a sales commission and we put the store on the market. After some false starts we got our sales price. Over time Mickey had learned all the details of the venture.

She was, in fact, the vice president of the Sub S Corporation. She attended the closing. Things were going well until the cousin of the buyer intervened and insisted the price was too high. I pointed out the written contract, but he was insistent. I got up, closed my briefcase and said, "Then there is no sale." The attorney for the buyer asked if the buyer's family could have a private conversation and I agreed. When they returned, the cousin was silent and the deal was closed. Mickey said later that when I stood up and closed my briefcase, her heart almost stopped because she thought I had blown the sale.

About a year later, our son opened another liquor store and asked if I would keep books for him. I agreed to do so for a token $100 a week. It was fortunate when we learned that a computer system like we had used was available at a bargain price in a St. Louis store. I picked it up and when it was in place we merely downloaded the bar code information that had been used in the old store.

When this store was sold two years later, the buyer asked if I would stay on and help him get established. It was November and I agreed to stay through the end of the year to familiarize him with the operation and to do his end of the year reports. The following February I gave my notice and went home and told Mick I had quit my job. Her response was, "Quit? Then you better get another. I can't have you under foot around the house. I have things to do!" I went back to the new owner and told him my wife would not let me come home and could I have my job back. He was delighted and I stayed with him for five years.

We Wiley's had some health problems. Macular Degeneration had taken away my central vision and I could no longer drive. My wife's asthma and arthritis problems increased and one morning there was a crisis. We had just awakened. She said, "Bob, I'm bleeding."

I walked around the bed and found her side of the bed and the carpet next to the bed soaked with blood. I could not stop the flow and called 911. The medics transported her to the hospital where they got the bleeding stopped. The condition is called a Venus Ulcer. It is caused by the sudden, unexplained burst of a vein in the calf of the leg. She had to return to the hospital on a regular basis to be treated by a wound specialist.

Now neither of us could drive. Fortunately the Regional Transportation District has a program where a person may call one to three days in advance and they will send a bus to take you to and from medical appointments. A great service.

It's funny how sometimes when things are not going well, a pleasant experience from the past will pop into your mind. One day my insurance man called and asked how would I like an additional $25,000 policy that didn't cost me anything. Yeah, right and the Easter Bunny leaves candy eggs. Then he explained that dividends had accrued since the policy was taken out when I built the miniature golf course in 1968. These funds were sufficient to pay the premiums on both the existing and the new policy. Now I had two policies paying dividends with no cash out of pocket. Do folks take good care of me or what?

During one of Mickey's frequent doctor visits, I mentioned that while walking five blocks up a slight incline I got tightness in my chest.

"You had a chest pain?" I assured the doctor there was no pain, just tightness.

"I think you should have a stress test." When I asked if that was absolutely necessary, she replied, "No, it's not ABSOLUTELY necessary. You're eighty-years-old. You have had a good life. Why worry about a little test?" Her sarcasm led to an echocardiogram, then to an angiogram. As she reviewed the test results she said I was losing blood.

I said, "How could I be losing blood? I have no blood in my urine or in my stool. I don't even have bleeding gums." She insisted that I have a colonoscopy. They discovered an extremely aggressive cancer. It was completely removed. Because of my doctor's persistence, it was discovered so early that it was entirely self-contained. It had not even penetrated the wall of the colon. I had neither chemo nor radiation. God bless that pushy, caring, competent little doctor.

After each of her numerous hospital confinements, Mickey was sent to a nursing home for rehabilitation. She hated that. She asked me to promise to do everything possible to make sure that she would never be confined to one of these facilities. I promised.

When she became bedridden, I was able to employ a visiting nurse. She came twice a week, examined and took vitals and reported to our family doctor. They worked very well together and gave my wife excellent treatment. Once a week, a practical nurse came in to bathe Mickey and massage her muscles. I hired a care giver to come each Sunday and stay with Mick while I went to church and had brunch with friends. I took a break every Thursday to play bridge with a group of retired men. During these times, we were blessed with a care giver named Theresa.

She took care of Mickey's personal needs, made lunch, cleaned house and folded the laundry that I had done. Most important, however, was how she would sit and talk to her ward. Mickey looked forward to these chats and they became close friends.

The morning of March 8, 2008, began like any other. We got up; I lifted my wife into her wheel chair and took her to the bathroom. I placed her on the stool and when she was finished I put on a fresh Depends which she required because of her incontinence. I lifted her back into her wheelchair and we went to the kitchen. I should mention here that the lifting was eased considerably by her weight loss. During an extended hospital stay she had had severe diarrhea and dehydration. She had gone from her normal 133 pounds to less than 100. We had breakfast and lingered as we chatted over cups of coffee. When we finished, I wheeled her to the bedroom. I stopped at the door and asked, "Honey do you want to stay up and watch TV or go back to bed?"

She did not answer. I walked to the front of the wheelchair. When I looked at her, her eyes were closed and she was slightly slumped. She was no longer suffering.

After the funeral, I continued to live in the patio home that we had purchased in 1993. The exterior maintenance, snow removal and front yard lawn maintenance were all taken care of by the homeowners' association. I was responsible for the backyard with the flower beds, small lawn area, and the fish pond. I had long ago hired a gardener to take care of the flower beds because my limited eyesight kept me from telling a weed from a flower.

I purchased an electric scooter. I used the sidewalks to go to Walgreen's, the bank, Lowe's, Safeway and several fast food outlets. I acquired a Visionary, a machine that enlarged printed material and showed it on a large monitor. I installed it in the office area of my basement. My independence was pretty much intact.

Our youngest son was one of the producers at the Denver Improv, a comedy club in north Denver. He said they had "open mike" nights where amateurs were allowed to perform. He encouraged me to try. I told him I knew nothing about standup comedy and did not even know were to start. He said that I should just talk about things I knew or saw. I wrote a "set" which was about two and a half pages. I gave them to him to edit. He returned them with notes like "not funny, this is a funny story, not a joke and not appropriate for your age."

My two and a half pages had been reduced to half a page. When I asked, "What do I do now?"

"Write some more," he said.

Finally I was ready for my debut. When I came on stage as "Grampa Bob" I got the usual mild applause greeting. My opening line was, "Thank you. I am happy to be here. At 84 I'm happy to be ANY where." From then on, I think the audience was on my side. At the end of my set, I was well received. I was invited to return in a couple of weeks. I did so with a somewhat edited script. Our son instructed me to be aware of lines that did not "work" and to replace them. Again, I was well received. This was kind of fun.

Some time later, I was invited to participate in a contest at the Denver Comedy Works, the premium comedy club in the Denver area. I was one of the winners in the first round. My daughter, who had attended with some friends exclaimed, "Dad, you are the only one who got a standing ovation."

I was elated. There were nine contestants in our division for the next round, each vying for a shot at the finals. I was not selected. After the show, the producer came up to me and said, "Wiley you did a great job. I know it is small consolation, but we are only advancing two and you placed third." I felt good that he would take time to convey his thoughts. Another thing that elated me was when a number of people from the audience came up to me and congratulated me on having a "family" set. I had purposely avoided using smut and four letter words. I was glad so many people appreciated the effort.

The experience was fun, but since I no longer drive it is too much of a hassle to arrange transportation for such a hobby.

In the fall of 2009, I was mowing the back yard lawn when I realized that I could no longer tell where I had mowed and where I had not. This caused some introspection. I consider my limited vision an inconvenience, but not a handicap. At the same time, the chances of tripping while using the stairs in my home were increased. If I fell, I could be seriously injured. With this in mind, I decided to sell my home. I talked to two real estate brokers and said I hoped to sell the following spring. Each pointed out that many owners do not want the hassle of the selling a house during the holidays and bad winter weather. As a result, the supply shrinks but the demand may continue. I decided to sell right away. Each broker gave me an estimated sales price and they were within a few hundred dollars of each other. In all my years in the real estate business, I came to the conclusion that no one can estimate a market price within five percent.

With that in mind, I listed the home at the price the brokers recommended, but in my mind I decided that an acceptable offer could be five percent less. I listed the home on October 30 and it closed on December 30 at a price within $1,000 of my mental target.

I do not recall any one of my children suggesting that I move into a retirement residence, although they may have.

What I do know is that each of the four applauded the decision I made. My son took me shopping for desirable quarters. Some we looked at were dismissed out of hand. Several were acceptable, but only one or two were really desirable. I settled on Garden Plaza of Aurora.

When people ask me how I like living there I say, "It may not be for everyone, but for me it is perfect." I have a two bedroom, two bath unit, with a nice living room and a complete kitchen and utility room with washer and dryer. I am on the fourth floor and have a balcony with a spectacular view. One bedroom I use as an office and a place to watch TV. I have a sofa bed for overnight guests and the second bath is adjacent. I describe the building décor as elegant without being pretentious. My fellow residents are, for the most part, open and friendly. There are those that resent being here and complain constantly. They are a minute minority.

The staff takes excellent care of me. They clean the unit once a week and launder the towels and bed linens. Residents are served a continental breakfast and we have the choice of lunch or dinner. I don't know what the additional fee is, but folks can have lunch and dinner. There are regular shopping trips and transportation is available to take us to doctor appointments. The facility is relatively new so, although there are many, activities are not particularly organized. One of the activities is the reason for this book. The president of the Colorado Independent Publishers Association lectured one afternoon and encouraged residents to write a poem, a short story or an autobiography.

One of the residents complained, "I have nothing to write about."

I challenged her. "What do you mean nothing to write about? Do you realize that the average resident here has lived one third as long as there has been a United States? We're thirty percent as old as our country. Think about it." After that confrontation, I thought *Wiley, are you just a blowhard or do you believe it?* That motivated me to sit down at the computer and start.

I have pointed out that I do not agree with my daughter's evaluation of my childhood. Even if her assessment were true, it would pale in light of the blessing and opportunities that I have been afforded during my lifetime.

LIFE IS GOOD!!

MICKEY AND BOB WILEY

CPSIA information can be obtained at www.ICGtesting.com
Printed in the USA
BVOW012211281011

274797BV00006B/4/P

9 781432 774332